The Story of Evan:
A Christian Novelette

By Robert Curtis and Steve Eggleston

DORRANCE
PUBLISHING CO
EST. 1920
PITTSBURGH, PENNSYLVANIA 15238

Dorrance Publishing Co
585 Alpha Drive
Pittsburgh, PA 15238
Visit our website at www.dorrancebookstore.com

ISBN: 979-8-88812-072-9
eISBN: 979-8-88812-572-4

Synopsis

This book tells the story of 21-year old Evan Anders, a recent Loyola University graduate uncertain about his Christian spiritual identity, who is seduced by the temptations of Lollapalooza, then falls in love with a girl he meets there, Delilah McChristie, who helps him through the troubled waters. In the process, they both come of age, choose to pursue a Christian life, and get engaged to be married.

The book starts with Evan having just finished college and moving back into his parents' home near Atlanta, which is also the home where he grew up, attended school and church, and spent most of his youth. Uncertain about many things like young people are, he's struggling with the one question that everyone keeps asking him: what does he want to do with his life? And even more importantly, who does he want to be? The book thus has undertones of the classic coming-of-age film, *The Graduate*, but is told in modern times in the context of Christianity.

One of Evan's Christian friends, Gary Canzone, is pulling further and further away from the church and invites Evan to attend Lollapalooza with him because his girlfriend has broken up with him and he has an extra ticket. Evan has never attended Lollapalooza, the epic four-day music festival in Chicago's Grant Park, and though considers resisting the temptation, he asks himself, "What can it hurt?" And because he loves music – he's played acoustic guitar for his church's worship team for the past 4 years – he decides to go.

Having made the decision to go, some of his friends are excited for him and wish they were going, "because everything and anything can happen there," while his friends from church caution against it for the very same reason. They think he should give the ticket back and instead join them at the revival where Kirk Franklin will be performing back home in Atlanta over the same weekend.

Evan doesn't want to disappoint his parents or his church friends so he comes up with a lie that he can't attend Lollapalooza or the revival because he must attend a financial services convention in Las Vegas in preparation for his upcoming exam.

On the way to the concert, having succumbed to the temptation of the big event he always wanted to attend as a kid, he is anxious and confused about what he really wants in life. This is compounded by his friend Gary Canzone's irrepressible urge to "get laid" over the next four days at the concert. Gary is definitely going through some hormonal issues as he is a closet porn addict who is constantly teasing Evan with the latest snippets that he shares on Snapchat so they quickly disappear.

After they park their car and make the long hike into the concert grounds, they are overwhelmed by all the people and excitement and general insanity that Lollapalooza is renowned for. The grounds are overwhelming because a small city has been tilted-up in a matter of days with hundreds of thousands of people in attendance, together with their tents, BBQs, and every-drug-known to man or woman. Neither of them has ever seen anything like it before, and though they are by no means tee-toddlers, this is far more than even they expected.

The guys find their reserved spot and pitch their tent, then start assessing the concert and figuring out where all the different bands are going to be playing. The wide array of talent includes Alternative Rock, heavy metal, punk rock, hip hop, electronica, R&B and soul, and even a few pop country bands. In fact, there are so many bands and stages that they don't know how they will ever see everyone they want to see. Right away both start circling and prioritizing their choices. Which is totally fun.

They grab a beer and as they look out over the whole of the massive festival grounds with its sea of heads that could an endless flock of gulls from the Aegean Sea back in the time of John of Patmos. Then Evan experiences the weirdest flash across his line of vision. As he looks at the stages and endless tents and people, he is struck by images from the Book of Revelation of the 7-headed dragon rising from one of the stages and 7 angels floating across the grounds like formed clouds with bowls in their hands.

His heart and mind in awe, he wonders to himself, "am I seeing what John saw in his vision when he wrote Revelation all that time ago? Pastor Jacobs said that God speaks to us in mysterious ways… is this it?" And before it is done, he could swear on a stack of bibles that he hears Jesus (or a male voice that he imagines might be Jesus), say, "Son, I am coming and there will be a Judgment Day. I am coming, so prepare your life and make your decisions accordingly…"

The vision comes to him just as he's relaxing from the beer, the sunshine and the atmosphere of celebration in the air, giving him at once a sense of spiritual ecstasy and deep anxiety. It's not that he loves porn, but he is a young man with male hormones and he had guiltily hoped he might meet a young lady and get laid, just as Gary has been talking about the whole drive there. Now he is stopped in his tracks because he knows that sex before marriage, strictly speaking, is a sin. So now this dilemma is like a dark cloud that may hover over his head the whole concert.

And making it worse, the festival has just begun and they have tickets for all four days with plans to sleep in their tent all three nights and have a great old time, including some moments that might not be remembered ;-). Now his mind is torn between having loads of fun and lots of beer and chasing girls or abstaining from the "desires of the flesh" and staying pure, as the Apostle Paul would encourage. He knows that in the past he has succumbed to porn or having sex outside marriage, but recently he had been doing better to get his thoughts under control. Now he has this throbbing dilemma, no pun intended.

He and Gary set upon the concert grounds and take in the experience, visiting various stages, watching the opening bands, eating hotdogs and burgers and drinking more beer, until by sunset they are sunburned and tired. When heading back to their tent to take a nap, Evan bumps into a girl who immediately catches his eye, spilling half of her fresh New Moon on the ground. She's attractive with light brown shoulder-length hair and big green eyes and has a bright smile on her face. He apologizes and offers to buy her another beer and she happily accepts, and the next thing you know they are jabbering away about everything from their favorite bands to what type of church they go to.

"I went to Maranatha High School just around the corner from my church. We were always rivals with this school named Bethany down the street. We always demolished them in football," she said with a smug laugh.

"What the heck! That's my school! You guys may have had the better football team, but we beat you in literally everything else," he teased, to which she rolled her eyes playfully.

"Ha ha, well, I didn't realize I had a Gladiator in my midst! I guess we can't be friends then."

With a smirk, she slowly starts to get up and doesn't resist at all when Evan takes her hand and pulls her back down, a little closer to him this time. Still holding hands, they lock eyes for a few seconds until Evan starts feeling self-conscious and clumsily breaks the silence.

"So um… what church did you go to?"

"I went to our Lady of Sorrows on Avalanche. Well actually I still go there every Sunday...But I mean, it's not *that* serious. I just go to listen to the homily and see some of my friends. What about you? What church are you at?"

"Faith Community on Lockwood."

"That's cool. How often do you go?"

The truth is that Evan goes to church every weekend as well, but has really been trying to take his faith seriously with what he does the rest of the week as well. But he doesn't want to seem too religious or uptight or serious to Delilah, fearing he might scare her away, so he just says, "Same as you. I go on Sundays but mostly just to see friends."

He senses a faint hint of disappointment in her reply, "oh, okay," almost as if she were wishing that he went to church more often. He wonders if maybe she held back on admitting how seriously she took her faith, just like him. Then after a few awkward seconds of silence, she declares, "OMG, we're at Lollapalooza, we have to take a freakin' selfie!"

Quickly she whips out her phone, going straight to Snapchat. For the next who knows how long they try on different Snapchat filters and Evan notices her face getting progressively closer to his as they take pictures. He feels proud that she's decided to put him on her story and notices that she's getting a lot of messages coming in from her friends in response.

Time goes on and all of a sudden the sun goes down. Evan glances at his watch and realizes that it's almost time for the Childish Gambino performance to start for the night on the main stage.

"Oh shit!" he yells. "It's almost nine. We gotta go!"

"Hmm," she says. "I don't know about you, but I'm going to the Ariana Grande performance! You coming?"

"What? Seriously? Heck no, I'm going to Childish Gambino… I can't believe you listen to her!"

"She speaks to my soul," Delilah says only half sarcastically.

"Ha ha, alright, alright, well, I have to get going. I guess I'll see you around?" He gives her an awkward hug and starts walking away backward, still looking at her.

Their time together had been so perfect that he was afraid to get her number for fear of disrupting the magic. If he leaves her now, this time will forever be perfect. She will forever be the perfect girl he met at the festival. And he's afraid of pursuing things more and then discovering that he's not as perfect and put together as he appeared to be during their time together.

"Yeah, I guess I'll see you around then," she says as she waves goodbye with a slight look of disappointment on her face.

They move further and further away from each other, each looking back to get last looks of each other, and soon enough they can't see each other through the crowd.

As Evan makes his way to the Childish Gambino stage, he is kicking himself for not getting her number. He came to this festival to have fun and let loose, and here comes this amazing girl and he couldn't even bring himself to get her number.

He grabs another beer and tries to shake away his regret by losing himself in the whole atmosphere of the festival. When he gets to Childish Gambino he sees and reconnects with Gary, who says, "Bro, where have you been? I figured you would have been back in our tent area by the time I woke up from my nap!"

"Oh, I've just been with Delilah."

"Delilah? That girl with the amazing ass?"

Evan felt kind of embarrassed but laughed and said, "I guess."

"So are you guys meeting up later?"

"Actually, I didn't get her number."

"Bro, are you serious?"

"I know, I know. Just leave it alone. Maybe I'll run into her again, and if not it wasn't meant to be."

"Whatever dude. You're crazy. ——Oh my gosh, there he is!"

Childish Gambino comes onto the stage and Evan takes his mind off of Delilah for a while and enjoys the concert until it is over.

Unable to resist, as soon as the show is over and he's out of the tightly packed crowd to looks at his phone to see if Delilah has messaged him. Instantly he sees he has an Instagram message from her and gets totally excited. Turns out he had come up on her Suggested Friends list because they had some mutual acquaintances due to their living in the same area.

Maybe it *is* meant to be, he thinks. He asks her how the Ariana Grande concert was and she replies "A lot better than your concert, I'm sure!"

"Ha ha, whatever," he replies, then with anticipation types, "You hungry?"

Instantly she replies, "Starving."

His heart explodes, they meet up, and for the next few days they spend lots of time with each other.

Between these occasions, however, Evan's bizarre vision returns and he attaches a bunch of bands to the from each of the seven genres of music to the different Christian sins.

It's a strange encounter each time, and after several days Evan thinks maybe it's the result of too little sleep, and he even entertains the notion that somebody might have spiked his Coke with drugs.

The most severe episode is when he's watching a death metal band and the numbers 6-6-6 are flashed across the stage. He wants to ask Delilah what she thinks but is afraid that she will think he is too weird or going crazy, so he keeps his bizarre thoughts to himself.

Evan has heard that the numbers 666 stand for the devil or porn and wonders if the whole festival is somehow the work of the devil, with all its excesses, rampant drug use, profligate sexual encounters, and lack of faith. He reflects on his grandparents, parents, Christian friends, and pastor and wonders what they would think if they knew he had lied and gone to Lollapalooza. To fight off the guilt, he has another beer, and then, finding Delilah, they both have a few more beers.

That night Evan and Delilah have a wonderful time together, lost in the moment, moving from stage to stage, and eventually losing track and having far more beer than either should have had...until they end up in his tent, where things progressively grow from kissing to sex.

Since neither intended on having sex with anyone at the festival, neither has brought any protection; but when they wake up in the morning to a brightly shining morning sun, Evan feels a slight pang of guilt — but not a hint of regret. It's not the most pious start to their relationship, but he thinks they might really have something.

God forgive me, and please let this work out, he prays silently to himself, not believing he's in his sleeping bag at Lolla F_N Palooza with this most amazing girl. And though neither knows the thoughts of the other, they both secretly wonder if this isn't the love-at-first-sight fairy tale that they've heard about since they were kids.

A humorous moment occurs when they suddenly realize that they are not alone in the tent. Apparently Gary also drank too much and had rolled up in a ball in the corner of the tent and is just as surprised as they are when he wakes up and sees them both partially naked. So the guy who came to the concert to get laid, didn't; and the guy who came with no expectation of hooking up, did. But now Evan must live with his decision. And his decision (and hers) will prove to have profound consequences.

Delilah says she has to go and meet up with her roommate who was at the concert with her, so she can clean up their stuff and go. Evan and Delilah set a date to get lunch when they are back in Atlanta and then excitedly keep texting each other all day, sharing memes about the festival with each other and making all kinds of gooey funny comments that are only made with first love and infatuation.

As Evan and Gary driving home, Evan starts to feel a bit sick to his stomach. It's either the long weekend or he's now realizing he must make up another lie about what he's been doing for the last four days (and where he met Delilah). His parents are both home in the kitchen when he walks in, causing his face to turn red (but since he's so sunburned, neither is the wiser).

Evan falls back on his old lie and claims he was at the Las Vegas financial planning convention and that it was great and yes he did gamble but just the nickel slots because everyone else did and yes he learned tons about financial services and yes it's still the field he plans to get a license in. Everyone seems to accept his explanation without suspicion...and then over the next days life returns to normal...except, of course, now he's chatting and messaging nonstop with Delilah, about whom he hasn't told anyone — yet.

Over the next couple of weeks he starts preparing for the financial licensing test that is scheduled for the next month, hangs out with his buddies who can't stop talking about the the revival, and starts to embrace the notion that maybe he and Delilah will become a serious item and that he'll have to openly talk about her and lie about how he met her. He's reminded of Luke 8:17: "For all that is secret will eventually be brought into the open, and everything that is concealed will be brought to light and made known to all." And every time he's so reminded, he just wishes the lying would end (though he can't stop).

Finally he gets up the courage to invite Delilah to church, and that's when he introduces his family to her for the first time. He says they met at the Las Vegas convention on financial services and she goes along with it, though she hasn't the slightest interest in pursuing that as a career. After church as they are walking to the park to join the family for the regular Sunday afternoon BBQ, he notices Delilah has gone quiet.

Earlier she said she needed to tell him something, but then people had gathered around them and she didn't have the chance. Then she lets go with the bombshell that she's pregnant, and he's totally stunned. All the things that flashed before him at the concert suddenly come back into his mind and he nearly faints. After sitting on a nearby park bench, he starts to gather himself and notices that Delilah is crying. His reaction obviously was not what she had expected.

For the first time in his life, he's utterly and totally speechless and can't even think. He's plain frozen.

When they return to the BBQ, everyone notices they are off. They give excuses but are both struggling with the situation and decide to leave early. They start talking about what they're going to do now and get on to the subject of what their family and friends will say...and the moment becomes overwhelming. Two young people, faced with a huge dilemma.

When Evan asks Delilah if she would ever consider an abortion, he can't believe the words even came out of his mouth. In fact he didn't mean to imply she should get one, but it must have sounded like that because she runs away in tears, gets in her car, and drives wildly away, almost hitting some kids crossing the street.

Head in a fog, Evan decides to walk home rather than go back to the BBQ and on the way Gary drives by and stops with a funny look in his face. He lives in the area and Evan wonders if he heard anything. But Gary has a funny look on his face and finally spills his guts, admitting he saw them have sex and has now connected the dots.

Gary gives Evan a ride home but when pressed Evan adamantly denies that Delilah is pregnant. Gary doesn't seem to buy it and now Evan realizes he's fallen into the trap of lying to everyone and knows he must confess to someone. That night he cannot sleep because the guilt is weighing so heavily on his soul, so the next morning he texts his old youth leader, Tim. They haven't talked in a while, but Tim was always there for him when he needed him and Evan knew he would be able to get everything out without being judged.

He decides to send a text. "Hey Tim! I know it's been a while but I have a lot going on and I could really use someone to talk to and give me wisdom. Do you have time to grab coffee in the next few days?"

Tim replies, "I'll pick you up tomorrow at 10."

The next day Tim pulls up and texts Evan, "Here!" and immediately Evan starts feeling knots in his stomach and sweating profusely. He's been holding in all of his secrets for so long, living under the burden of his lies for so long, and now the time has come to actually tell someone. He takes a deep breath, reaches out his shaky hand to open the front door, and walks out to meet Tim who is standing outside leaning against his car.

"What's up, man? I miss you. Thanks for reaching out," Tim says as he walks up to Evan and gives him a big hug.

"Thanks for saying yes," Evan says sheepishly.

"Of course. Starbucks?" Tim suggests.

"Sure, that sounds good."

They get to Starbucks and are lucky enough to find a comfy couch seat in the corner of the room. After ordering drinks, they sit down and there is a long silence as Tim waits for Evan to speak. But Evan is so nervous, he doesn't say anything. Finally Tim decides to break the ice and says, "So...what's going on, man? Tell me what's up."

Evan's voice starts off shaky as he is so nervous to reveal everything he has been holding in. Then he begins to pour out everything that he's been feeling, starting off with the burden and the stress that he's been under and then proceeding to the guilt that he feels and how far away from God he feels and how he's been trying to figure out the right way to live...but that he's been giving in to so many temptations. He talks about his struggle with pornography and lying, about going to the concert, about his visions of 6-6-6, and then finally about Delilah. He tells Tim he thinks he's in love but that's he's ruined it. He got her pregnant and didn't mean to suggest abortion, but that's how she took it and now she hates him, or maybe she does. He does not know. She just ran away crying.

Tim asks him, "So, what do you want?"

"What do you mean, what do I want?"

"I think you need to ask yourself what do you really want? Do you want to be free? Do you want to keep living under the burden of your lies and your secrets and your shame, or do you want to step into the freedom that God has for you? It's your choice, you know."

Evan takes a second to think and after taking a deep breath, exhales and gushes, "I want to be free."

"Alright then," Tim says with a warm smile. "We can work with that. If you're willing to take the steps to get free, God can take care of the rest. Can I pray for you?"

Evan agrees and Tim places his hand on Evan's back and prays. He asks God to take off Evan's burdens, to take away any shame, any fear, anything that's holding Evan back from being close to God.

As Tim prays, Evan feels a warmth in his body, and physically feels a weight being lifted off of his shoulders. By the time Tim is done praying, Evan feels a lightness of being and a freedom in his spirit that's like rapture.

"Wow. Thank you," Evan says with a huge smile on his face that he can't contain.

"My pleasure," Tim says, patting Evan assuredly on the back. "Remember that God loves you, his grace is sufficient for you, and he forgives you. All he wants is for you to live the life he's created for you to live."

"Yeah, I just needed to be reminded of that," Evan admits sheepishly.

"Love you, bro."

They hug and Tim brings life back to focus. "So, now that we've found a true path, what are you going to do about Delilah?"

"I don't know," I mean, I don't want her to get an abortion. I'll keep the baby even if she doesn't want it. But what I really want is to just be with her and figure it out together, you know?" He pauses and as he does a wave of panic spreads across his face.

"Oh no — Do you think she could be going to get an abortion right now?" Evan asks, naïve as to how the whole process works.

"I don't know," Tim shrugs. "You know her better than I do."

"Okay, we've gotta go! I need to go find her right away!"

He jumps up, grabs his jacket, and rushes out the door, Tim close behind him. As they get in the car, Evan anxiously fumbles with his phone and calls Delilah. It goes straight to voicemail. He calls again and again, but no answer. Then he pulls up Instagram and sends her a message, "Delilah. Please. I need to talk to you."

Tim drops him off at home and they hug and say goodbye. Evan gets into his own car and rushes over the Delilah's apartment and knocks on the door. He cracks his knuckles nervously as he waits. The door opens and he sees Delilah's roommate who he met at Lollapalooza, standing in pajamas and slurping up some Top Ramen.

"Hey, um, is she here?" Evan asks earnestly.

"Delilah? I haven't seen her since yesterday. She just grabbed her phone charger and her laptop and left. I thought maybe she was going somewhere with you."

"No, she wasn't with me," Evan replies with sadness. "Thanks anyway."

"Anytime," Delilah's roommate says, closing the door with her foot as she takes another slurp of her Top Ramen.

Feeling defeated and out of options, Evan gets back in his car and drives home. All he can do now is hope and pray that God makes a way for things to work out.

Days pass and still Delilah doesn't answer any of his calls or messages. One night as he lays in bed depressed, scrolling through Snapchat stories, he notices that Delilah's story has a posting from just a few hours prior. Eagerly he clicks on her story, only to be disappointed that it's just a quick picture of a gray speckled cat. Then he remembers — she had told him about her mom's cat! Knowing this would maybe be his only chance to figure out where she was, he grabs his car keys and heads to the place he had dropped her off after their first lunch date after Lollapalooza. Maybe it was her mom's place and he would find her there.

In the meantime, in his own mind he knows he has only one choice, and that is come clean to this family, ask Delilah to marry him, and have the child. He has loved her since first sight and she hinted at the same. So he finds peace in his decision, even if the timing of the question has been prompted by her pregnancy. It is still true and still the right thing to do.

Evan arrives at what he assumes is Delilah's parent's house, and runs up to the door and knocks. A woman answers the door and he realizes that he doesn't know who she is – mother, aunt, friend – because he's never met her family. She has shared some pictures, but he cannot place the face. He asks if Delilah is home and the woman says she's gone to visit her Aunt on the other side of Atlanta across the train tracks.

When he asks if Delilah is alright, the woman gives him a hard look and seems to connect some dots herself and says, "are you Evan whose name rhymes with heaven?" He flushes at her words and says he guesses so but wouldn't be so presumptuous to use his name in the same sentence with heaven, at which point the woman gushes that she is Delilah's other aunt and that Delilah has told her everything.

He practically faints for the second time that day and once again is speechless until the words blurt out, "I want to ask her to marry me and I want us to have the child and live a Christian life."

"Evan whose name rhymes with heaven," she says, "you better get a move on because she's gone to her aunt's, my sister's, to be taken to the doctor tomorrow to discuss having an abortion." She gives him the address and he puts it into his GPS and he thanks her.

Evan drives across Atlanta like a madman and is lucky to get to Delilah's aunt's house alive. When he races up to the door and knocks, breathless, a man answers and looks at him with disbelief because Evan knows he must look like a crazy man. After he explains who he is and why he is there, the man says he's Delilah's uncle and invites him into the living room. Turns out he's a pastor of his church but is interdenominational and they aren't against abortion: "the choice must be with the girl," he say s.

About that time he hears voices and it's obviously Delilah and her Aunt returning from somewhere. When Delilah sees Evan she equivocates between breaking into tears and flying into a rage of anger until he hugs her and says he loves her, at which time she just sobs with apparent happiness. Then the Aunt and Uncle depart, leaving them alone. Now is clearly the time Evan must step up to the plate and be a man, take responsibility for his lies and actions and, equally importantly, own his faith.

"I have a lot of things to say to you, but mostly I want to say that I don't want to keep up all the lies… I really want to live my life for God, every day, not just on Sundays… and I want to do it with you," he confesses.

But before he can continue, she interrupts. "That's what I want too!," she says. "I was afraid that you wouldn't be interested in me if I showed you how much I really want to take my faith seriously… and that fear led me to making some really dumb choices. We're here now and can't change what's happened… but I want to go forward making the choices God wants me to make… and I want to make them with you, too."

"Man… So you mean if we had just been honest with each other, we could have helped each other grow closer to God instead of everything that's happened," he says, to which she replies, "How crazy is that?"

He sees a decorative bauble on a table, grabs it and drops to a knee, whereupon he clumsily asks her to marry him." It's a heart-rending and poignant moment.

She hesitates - to create a little tension - then tays, "Yes, but on two conditions: One, we both put God first in our relationship from this point on, and two," she pauses and lets out a laugh, "you have to promise that you're changing diapers with me."

Evan laughs and says, "Deal."

He puts the bauble onto her finger and they hug. When the long, long, long hug ends, they look at each other and at the same say: "Oh, God, now we've got to tell your parents and grandparents the truth before Jesus returns to earth."

And that is the story of Evan whose name sounds like heaven.

Chapter 1: School's Done

The Class of 2019 were all Millenials, kids born on or near the turn of the century when the Reverend Jerry Falwell predicted God would pour out his wrath at the tick of midnight, 1999-2000. But while that hadn't happened, he'd led a new political movement known as the moral majority until his death in 2007. And though Reverend Falwell was largely unknown and thus irrelevant to the 2019 graduating class of the University of Chicago, all of them had grown up on computers, which had also been predicted to malfunction at midnight 1999-2000, causing a global crash and unimaginable catastrophes worldwide. That too didn't happen, and now here they all were, entering a world of troubled waters, to say the least.

Troubled waters were not on their minds at this exact moment, however, because the Class of 2019 were anxiously taking their designated seats inside the cavernous Joel L. Limond Auditorium. The place was packed with students, parents and families, a mix of elation and nervousness common for such occasions and punctuated by more perfume and cologne than Sunday church back home. At least that's how Evan Anders saw it, his stomach churning as he fought back nausea, not from the sickly sweet fumes entering his lungs, but because he had been procrastinating and that procrastination, in exactly two hours, would be over. He would graduate with a B.S., he thought snickering - *total B.S.* - in Business, with no idea what he was going to do with his life.

"Heavy!" a shrill voice rang out from somewhere in the direction of the C's, two rows of seats over and to his right, stage left. He whipped his head around as his eyes naturally scanned for his best friend in college, Gary Canzone, whose high-pitched voice might have landed him in the girls' choir back home in Elderpark, a tiny southern town outside "Atalanta," as Gary jokingly articulated it in some ridiculous faux southern accent he would conjure up, as if he knew how southerners talked and sounded, which he most definitely did not (he was born in upper New York). Yet he was cool, a balance of what mattered, which is what made them brothers of a different mother, he and Evan, hence the reference to heavy, you know the song lyrics, "you're not heavy, you're my brother").

"Duderonomie," Evan screamed back just loud enough to penetrate the boisterous din of voices yapping excitedly around him, in reference to the Book of Deuteronomy.

"The Lord is One!" Gary replied raising a finger and waving it wildly then lifting his square graduation cap into the air and giving the tassel a playful whirl.

"Attention, everyone," a deep booming voice suddenly said, turning all heads to the front and bringing a hush to the room. On stage a tall block-shouldered man who might have been Lurch in the old *Adam's Family* television show was dipping his chin toward a microphone which he now grasped in his hand, removed from its mic stand rack, and pulled to his mouth. "Test, test...Please be seated, we are ready to begin the graduation ceremony for the esteemed Class of 2019."

Esteemed might be a stretch, Evan thought with a snort. In fact, esteemed *was* definitely a stretch, because the class, if truth be told, had been downright blasphemous. A whole swath of jocks had been investigated for cheating on their midterms under the dark cloud of allegations that some Russian kid's father had engaged hackers from back home to steal the exams before the tests were given, or had changed the grades, or something vague like that, as was so typical of rumors in those days. And then Mueller had let Trump off, largely, and the whole thing just seemed to disappear. Evan now saw most of their big jock heads protruding above their peers as if nothing had happened; but everyone knew. Everyone.

But that wasn't all. The big thing had been the whole porn fiasco. It had taken place right there on the floor above his own in the Green Wing Dorms. The Green Wing was mostly for seniors who were not jocks, not playing any sports or anything like that, and were not nerds, not the really smart ones, and not lab rats either. Really the Green Wing was for everyone who didn't fit a niche, what you might call "normal" guys, if there even was such a thing. Not too smart, not athletic, not too political and not in a fraternity. Maybe people you didn't know where to put. That was normal, wasn't it? People you didn't know where to put, who didn't fit anywhere else? The future of the new American middle class.

Evan lifted his graduation hat, or was it a cap, he thought. But why would they call it a cap? It looked nothing like a baseball cap, more like a box top, if you asked him. He rubbed the cold perspiration from his close-cropped hair and adjusted the box-hat back on, wiping his sweaty hand on his pants and looking nervously back toward his family, hoping his dad hadn't seen him do that, or heard him yell to Gary. He didn't really know why he had that momentary pang of guilt. He just did. Maybe from the way he'd been brought up, religious and all, not Catholic but tightly wound. He even had a great Uncle who was Amish. Which was weird. At least he thought it was weird.

He waved to his mom who was indeed looking at him while waving feverishly as if he was on one of those big ocean liners about to pull away from the docks and take young men to war. To war. That's how his mind thought sometimes, especially when he was nervous like today. Thinking to movies he'd watched over the years. He didn't know why his mind was like that. It just was. It thought of things by reference to what he'd seen, what he'd been exposed to. And he liked war movies as a kid, watched a ton of them, even the black and whites ones, you remember? *Battle of the Bulge* starring, starring, ah, shit, he couldn't remember. Tony Curtis or Jim Wayne or somebody. Guys who were dead now, but his dad had talked about them like they were gods or something. Maybe that's why they came to mind. Because they were like God or something.

With a thin smile, he waved back to his mom, just a single wave and quickly turned back around happy his dad hadn't been looking his way. Already the guy who had called the room to order was gone and now the first row in front of him, the A-a's through the A-f's, were lining up and dancing across the stage. Names were being called and screams were erupting from the hall as families cheered on the great success of their sons and daughters for graduating from college with a manure mound of student loan debt that would, would, would, sink a ship. Gawd, he would have to stop thinking in metaphors every time he thought. Especially mixed ones, but he couldn't help himself; it was a curse. And Gary had the curse too. They were both cursed that way. Which made listening to their conversations pretty ridiculous sometimes.

Suddenly he noticed the girl next to him was gone and he looked over and already she was walking up the aisle and the guy on the other side of him was yapping loudly, "hey, hey, hey, Evan, you gotta go, hey—" so Evan did go and bumped a few chairs he was moving in such a hurry and even bruised his thigh and then he caught up and everything was fine but he was sweating profusely and drops of perspiration - water really, if you asked him - were running like rivers across his face and he wiped them off like a cowboy in the hot sun riding a broncho until...finally he took his diploma and shook the man's hand. He recognized this man but couldn't remember his name and thought why didn't he wear a name tag, well, that would be stupid, but smiled anyway and turned and looked at his mom and dad who now were both standing and smiling and hooting like he was about to score a touchdown or something, though he didn't play football. And his dad, he usually never screamed. So this was a big moment. And it made him feel swell, really, really swell. Maybe even proud.

But the swellness soon wore off because he was in the A's, which meant all the B's through the Z's - there were three Z's he thought, Zadon and Zemeke and a kid whose name sounded like the animal, ah, ah, Zebra - and all of them still had to go, which was the curse of having a last name that started with "A." Sure, it meant that he went first, which was good for things that were good, or things you wanted to get out of the way, but it also meant you had to wait a long time for everyone else to go for a lot of things, and when he had to wait his mind naturally wandered. Which reminded him, or gave him time to be reminded, about the porn scandal which had turned into a fiasco because, hell, the whole floor had almost gotten kicked out of the school. Except they didn't because no one could prove who did it. and because they were jocks, always getting special treatment And because no one could prove who did it, and everyone couldn't have done it, so everyone got off the hook. Well, not off the hook, but not expelled.

All those guys were here too, the big heads and clunks and idiots, if you asked him, most of them. And he knew many of them pretty well because they too were a bunch of normal guys, with the one exception of course. That exception being the someone on that floor who, in direct violation of the dorm room code of ethics, had hacked into the system and enabled everyone on the floor to watch porn if they wanted to. And apparently many of them did, because the draw on the band width is what got someone from cyber-security to go snooping around and see a literal ton of it had been downloaded to stuff. So maybe, on second thought, the guy who had hacked the porn was normal, too, even if he had a big head.

Yeah, if he thought about it, which he did because they were only on the P's by now, if he thought about it, well, there was lots of sin all around him. Not just the cheating on exams and the porn. Lots of it. Everywhere. So what am I going to do about it? he chuckled. Nothing, that's what you're going to do. Nothing. Plain nothing. And therein laid the problem. There was sin all around him and he had no plan of what to do about it or what to do with his life. Yeah, and what was that saying? You know the one. It goes, "Idleness is the devil's workshop," or something like that. No, it's idle hands, "idle hands are the devil's workshop," or is it minds, or the playground.

Hell, he couldn't really remember, but Evan, friend of Gary - cause he ain't heavy he's my brutha, Gary - was about to enter the world with nothing but idleness to occupy him. Which might not be a good thing. Unless you're the devil looking down, smiling.

Chapter 2: Look Homeward

He thought in book titles too, and as his dad's Ford Explorer hummed down the highway he was thinking of that book with 'homeward' in the title, you know the one, by Thomas Wolfe, Wolfe with an e, *Look Homeward, Angel.* He was thinking about this because Gary had come home with him for Christmas break when they were juniors, and after seeing his house, Gary had commented, "Dude, your house is right out of *Look Homeward, Angel*, like that Gant house in the book and that, I read, was like the real Wolfe house when he was growing up."

Evan had almost punched Gary at the time, for some reason, he didn't know exactly why, but he had, and though he had restrained himself he had been mad at Gary and thus Gary was mad at him for virtually the whole of the trip. Which had made them both miserable because it's hard to have fun on vacation when two guys are mad at each other. But, you know, Evan was thinking to himself as his dad turned down their street and he saw their house, Gary was right: their house did remind him of the Gant house, because ever since he left for college his parents were always renting out his bedroom, which was a garage that they had restored and converted, pretty cool, detached from the main house, and they had rented it to AirBNB types.

And not just the house was like book, he'd often thought. His whole town was a lot like Asheville, the fictional town in the Wolfe book that isn't so fictional. Of course the times were not the same. It was not the 1930's, with existence wedged precariously between two world wars, in the throes of the Great Depression, and of course the people in the book didn't know there would be a second world war but Wolfe did when he wrote the book, which may explain how dark it was, because Wolfe had been looking back with 20/20 hindsight. Or maybe it wasn't so dark as it was real, like today. I mean, today alcoholism isn't the problem. Well, not the main one. It's oxy and opioids and before that it was meth and before that, well, alcohol, because in a small town which his town was, people were bored.

And boredness means idleness.

"Home!" his dad Felder Anders announced from the driver's seat. He was a man who stated the obvious, of average height and build, prematurely balding not that it mattered anymore. Or perhaps that's what all parents did — state the obvious all the time ad nauseum.

"Oh, it's so wonderful to have you home, son," his mother added, not so obvious as it was repetitive. She had already said it a dozen times on the flight and then the drive home, except she had used coming, "it's so wonderful to have you *coming* home." And now here they were no longer coming, having arrived.

"Is my room—"

"Yes, honey," his mom interjected, obviously knowing where the question was headed. "You have your room all summer, or as long as you want it. How long will you stay?" she again asked, as if she hadn't asked him several times already, which is something else parents did, his in particular. Ask the same question over and over again, no matter how many times it was answered or couldn't be answered, as if asking it again would generate a different response.

"Not sure, mom. As I said earlier, I've got to figure out what I'll be doing."

His dad's door slammed and he took the signal and they all retrieved their suitcases and dispatched to their rooms, agreeing to collect in the kitchen for dinner in several hours. After his dad handed him the key and patted him on the back he himself into his garage room and stood there, looking around to see if anything had changed. It was obviously a converted garage because you could see the rafters, but that was more for effect - "its very rustic," his mom would say to potential renters - and the place was complete with a kitchen, bathroom and shower, and living room with a couch that opened up into a bed. A large flat screen covered the far wall too with a remote wired to the coffee table so it would not be taken, accidently. And his posters, they were still on the walls, held up by thumbtacks.

He punched the on button of the remote, and as he did a massive blast of Wolf Blizter filled the screen and his ear drums at the same time and it all felt chaotic when his mobile also started humming and spinning round the coffee table where he'd laid it. He answered before silencing Blitzer which he would have done anyway, "brutha Gary, how's the Good Lord treating you today now that you've joined the legions of the most debt-ridden student graduates in U.S. history?"

"Please don't even bring that up, Heavy, 'cause like you I've got no job prospects but, unlike you, I have something else of great value."

"You do, what's that?"

"Three guesses my friend, and if you guess right, you win a prize."

Evan sat on the sofa and placed his phone on the coffee table after tapping speaker. "Well," he said as he fumbled in his interior coat pocket for the cigar that he'd bought himself in a moment of celebratory glee. Then before he finished his thought he snapped a lighter from the table, probably there to light candles, took several puffs, blew out the smoke. "Well, I'll have to cogitate on that invitation for a moment, since so much is at stake."

"I'm going to have to put on a clock," Gary said, "on account of I don't have all day like you apparently do."

"Thought you said you were jobless, like me."

"I am, but I'm not derelict, like you," he jested, then busted out laughing.

"Susie Ann Mohr called you and wants to get back together," Evan said, changing directions. Susie was Gary's heartthrob beginning back in high school but who had recently dumped Gary for some rich kid from the lakes.

Gary snorted loudly, putting a grin on Evan's face because he too had eyes on Susi. If Susie wasn't going with Gary anymore, maybe the lake kid would be a false starter and she'd get together with him. Not entirely unreasonable for a young man his age, he thought, because all is fair in love and war.

"Clock's ticking," Gary said. "I'm serious. I have places to go before the sun sets."

"Your grandpa offered to pay off all of your college loans give you a free all-paid summer trip to Europe because you're the biggest spoiled brat I know," Evan said with a snort.

"Boy, don't I wish," Gary replied. "Don't I wish."

Hmm, Evan thought to himself. He was half serious with the last guess, because Gary's dad was filthy rich, rubbed elbows with Pence and Trump and had some massive estate in Boca Raton. Ah, that's it. "Same said grandad offered you a job at his Fort Lauderdale golf resort for the summer kissing rich asses and leering at lots of cleavage."

"Wrong, wronger, and wrongest," Gary said. "Three strikes and you're out."

"Out of what, jerk wad. Stop messing with me, okay? Because you know and I know it that you're just pulling my leg because if there's some fun involved and you've got like tickets to something I'm going to be the one going with you. Simple as that."

A loud rip of laughter erupted from the other end.

"Tickets, it's tickets," Evan said. "You've got tickets to something, and you know what, that first guess didn't count anyway. It was just a tester, not a real guess. You have tickets to, to, to—"

"Lollapalooza, dude! I won tickets to 'palooza! And since Susie doesn't know what she's lost, I'm going to hook up with every girl I can meet over three days."

Evan was caught off guard by this one, all teasing and silliness aside. He'd seen his friend pulling further and further away from the church and this was just another example of his licentious direction. Evan took a reflective puff of his cigar and contemplated what to say, because truth be told he'd never been to Lollapalooza despite four years at UOC and had always wanted to go.

"Do I hear silence?" Gary said. "Do I hear a man hesitating to go to the most epic music concert on the face of the planet with his best friend who just won tickets on the radio for all four days, all expenses paid, not to mention backstage passes to the main stage and epic pics with the headliners?"

A rap at the door broke him from the grip of indecision.

"Evan, dinner," came his mother's voice from behind the door.

Before college she would have barged in, insensitive to his privacy, but an embarrassing moment in his senior year - when she'd caught him watching porn doing the nasty - had cautioned her approach because it had embarrassed her more than him, though he had been embarrassed at dinner that night, hoping to God she hadn't told his father.

"Coming, mom!" Evan yelled, then he returned to Gary. "Look, you know I'm trying to get back closer to God and stuff, so I don't know 'palooza's exactly the best idea for—"

"Getting closer? Isn't he like...everywhere? How can you get closer if—"

"Yeah, look, not like physically closer. I don't mean that literally, dinglebat, obviously. I just need to think about it. It's not what I had in mind for my summer."

"Had in mind? You don't have anything in mind. Isn't that our mutual problem?"

"I don't know. Let me pray about it."

Chapter 3: Lead Us Not Into Temptation

You could say the city of Elderpark was defined by its churches. For a city of 29,000 residents - 40,000 at its heyday in the 1970s - it had more churches per capita than any city in America except maybe Ashland, Kentucky. Churches of every denomination, though mostly evangelical, dotted streets and neighborhoods from top to bottom — top being literally the high side of the city, altitude 1000 feet above sea level, bottom being literally the low side of the city, where the railroad tracks snaked alongside the muddy Tillerman River.

With so many churches, faith was the lifeblood of the people. Episcopalians, Methodists, and Baptists primarily, but also a single Catholic church and one synagogue, all surrounded by what seemed like tilt-up non-denominationals because a new one seemed to sprout up every other month until about ten years ago, when a balance was found, of populace, faith, and churches all fitting each other's needs. Evan and his family were Episcopalians, who valued a high liturgy and deep commitment to faith, somewhere between the intensity of Baptists and Catholics.

It was the first Sunday since his arrival home on a Wednesday and he still hadn't worked out the answer to Gary's invitation to Lollapalooza. He was still on the fence, his indecision now complicated by several other things, and as he exited his garage room wearing his Sunday three-piece, a blue-striped suit, button-down vest, and tie, he had already decided he'd pray on it one final time today and make a decision. "I'll walk if you don't mind," he said to his parents, who were already in the car waiting, engine running, windows down as the morning cool was already giving way to another balmy spring day in the south.

"Sure, honey," his mother said, her elbow bent on the window sill. And with that, his dad backed up and meandered down the road and he set upon his walk of half dozen blocks, mostly along the east side of the city's central park. He once knew all the neighbors on both sides of the street, as he'd moved there when he was in kindergarten. Thinking he might recognize someone, he paused here and there looking for cars his friends drove in high school, but saw none that registered. Time was like a leaf-blower, he thought, an invisible but powerful force that pushed things into a pile that was swept up, bagged, and stored elsewhere, out of sight except for memories.

Why didn't I ride my scooter, he thought to himself as he reached the park, where a dozen kids were zipping around on theirs. He loved the freedom that his longboard had brought him, the speed, grace, and jumps. "Wow," he said aloud as a kid did a full 360 off the high lip. He'd never gotten that good because he'd never put in the time. Kids like that do it for the passion, for the thrill, for the ecstasy of it. And there it was, he thought, the nub of the quagmire in which he found his life. Nothing stirred his passion the way that jump stirred that kid's. Except maybe one thing. Just one thing. A calling to God, but that seemed so, so, so — remote, despite him being everywhere. It wasn't like he'd attended seminary or anything.

A bit angry with himself, Evan kicked a rock and sent it bouncing into the street, skipping up and grazing the side of a passing car. He cringed for a moment but the driver didn't seem to notice so he quickly moved on to a tinge of guilt. He felt guilt. Because he wanted to go 'palooza. And what he really needed to decide was whether he'd go to that decadent concert with Gary, whose proclaimed purpose was to get laid by as many women as possible, or not. And if not, maybe miss a once-in-a-lifetime opportunity. He smiled, thinking, it wouldn't be the end of the world, would it? To get laid. After all, he did indulge porn himself, guiltily, occasionally, but he wanted to put that behind him. He really did.

A bunch of his old Christian friends from high school had that morning included him in a group Instagram chat, kids from his church club, and all were going to a Christian concert in Florida with some big Christian bands headlining that he'd seen a million times but still loved. So he had a choice, go to Lollapalooza or that concert...actually there was also the third, more responsible choice. His dad had offered to pay for him to attend a Financial Services convention in Las Vegas of all places, where the purpose was to help recent graduates take their licensing tests, which was vaguely his plan. To take the financial licensing test that summer and start to work in the fall.

It had vaguely been his plan for nearly a year, but it was really not a plan, just a fall back. An option if nothing else better came along. What he would do if he couldn't think of anything else. He certainly wasn't passionate about it. It would make him money and with his license he could go to work for someone locally whom his dad or mom would refer to him or that he knew from the church. And that reminded him, he wanted to say hey to Bill Smith, who sang in the choir and ran the financial services group in nearby Pinstone, population 250,000, only half hour commute away. Bill was about ten years older than him but their fathers were friends, went fishing together sometimes, and he had a son, but his son wasn't going into finance. He had moved to New York to become a musician. Something crazy like that. Yet if he did get that license, that's the first place he'd apply. To Bill Smith's.

Suddenly the birds started chirping loudly now, or he just noticed them for the first time, maybe they were announcing that the church was coming up on the left and that he needed to cross the street. He looked both ways and trotted across, jaywalking being common here in small town America. And now he could hear the church bell tolling and announcing that ten o'clock services were about to begin. He was running late so he'd catch Smith afterwards when everyone hung around the steps saying hello and catching up on gossip before going to the BBQ in the park, which was perfunctory. Everyone went, usually. So that was his plan today, after church, unless something else came up, which it wouldn't.

The service was packed, ten in the morning being the most popular, and he couldn't find his parents until his mom turned around and waved. Same as at the graduation. She always waved that way. Sort of like the lady in *The Truman Show*. Growing up, his life had been sorta like that show, if he thought about it. *The Truman Show*. Every day the same thing happened, repeated itself, spun around and around with nothing changing. Well, not nothing, but mostly nothing, and he even wondered if he wasn't part of some big experiment, you know, where God was watching his flock and seeing what they were doing and what they would do next when challenged. Which is where he was. Challenged.

The worship band was concocted of a hodge-podge of volunteers from the church, including a high school kid slightly off beat and obviously still learning to play the drums; his buddy from his old high school band, on guitar, adding a little too many rifs like he always did, trying too hard or something; an older woman with a strong vibrato who was past her prime singing years; and a few more on keys, bass and background vocals — all crowded together on stage in the middle of leading the congregation in a mediocre but passionate rendition of "How Great Is Our God."

As Evan made his way down the aisle between the pews, self-conscious as ever, trying his best to ignore the side glances of people who were keenly aware that he had missed the first few minutes of worship, he saw Pastor Christy standing in the front row on the right side of the pews, arms appropriately raised just a foot above her thighs, hands shoulder-width apart, palms open, indicating she was giving her all to God and open to receive what He was saying.

Evan liked her, which put his mind at ease because he had experienced several who bugged him at his church in college. They would go on and on about all the vices of the day, which were many, talking about technological addiction sucking time, energy, and brain cells from Millenials, anything to do with sex or whatever, watching "Game of Thrones," the perils of drugs, and on and on and on and on. They were more concerned about what not to do and about saving face than inspiring what to do. If he were a pastor, that's what he'd do: inspire what to do, not what not to do. But Pastor Christy was different, which is why he liked her and would model himself after her. Genuine. Of course she would be honest and upfront with you, and she didn't sugarcoat the need to identify sin in your life and urge you to turn away from it… but she was less concerned with keeping you on your toes and making a checklist and more concerned with making sure you felt at home with her, God, and the church. Which he liked.

Evan continued down the long, crowded aisle making his way awkwardly past the knobby knees and scooting past the first five people in his parents' row, because of course they couldn't have just taken seats at the end. He made the necessary quick, whispered apologies as he bumped into more knees and forced people to scoot one way or the other to let him through. Even though everyone was by now standing up, he took a seat. *I'm sure God has more important things on his mind than whether I'm standing or sitting during worship*, he thought. And eventually the music came to an end and was followed by a lengthy prayer delivered by the worship leader, noticeably accompanied by piano in the background. Then Pastor Christy made her way onto the stage and everyone else sat down in their pews.

As much as Evan tried, and no matter where he went, he had always had a difficult time concentrating during sermons. He tried to use the fill-in-the-blank outlines that the church provided in their bulletins, but his mind always ended up wandering elsewhere. And this day, in particular, his mind was pulled toward the dilemma of accompanying Gary to the festival, going with his church friends, or, last on his list, going to the financial seminar. *If I go to Lollapalooza, maybe I can just be there as a good influence. There's no harm in that, right? Gary needs someone there to help tame him down a bit... Plus, what are the chances that I'm gonna meet someone and actually get laid anyway?* He found some blank space on his bulletin, pulled a pencil out of its slot in the back of the pew in front of him, and drew a table with two columns. *Pros... help a friend make good choices... meet new people...do something interesting for the first time in a long time...hear great music...God will always forgive me if I happen to end up making some bad choices. Cons...will have to lie to parents...miss the Christian music festival...will have to spend a lot more money, because food at festivals ain't cheap... may end up making some poor choices...*

"...and lead us not into temptation, but deliver us from evil. Amen," whispered Pastor Christy solemnly as she ended her sermon with the Our Father prayer and walked off the stage, leaving Evan worrying that he should have paid just a little bit more attention to what she was saying. He looked back down at the sheet of paper he'd been writing on, trying to make out what the fill-in-the-blanks were that had been printed beneath his scribbles, but he couldn't see enough to figure out the main points of what she'd shared. He took a second to clear his mind, took a deep breath, and brought his attention back to his dilemma. *God, what should I do? Please help me make the right decision.* Evan waited a few seconds for some sort of awesome, Spirit-filled moment of clarity to come to him, before getting bored, discouraged, and restless. *I guess if I didn't hear anything...then God's cool with it? I'm sure everything will be fine, and you know you'll regret not going, dude. And if it ever gets out that you went to the festival, you can just say you were there to help Gary make good choices like a good brother in Christ.*

Evan pulled out of his back pocket his Iphone 10+ complete with Otterbox case which he owned because he couldn't deny he was a klutz, slid it down his leg and tilted it up just slightly, trying to use it as subtly as possible and hiding it to the left of his bulletin so his mom wouldn't notice. Face recognition was a little difficult with the angle so he just put in his code and opened up iMessage. Gary's contact picture was from all the way back in 2015, face fuzzy before he needed to shave, taken during orientation weekend at school, with two not-so-subtle red cups in his hands and a pair of douchey sunglasses on. He hadn't evolved much. Evan felt a jab in his rib and looked up to his mother's eyes cutting into him like razor blades.

"Put your phone away!" she whispered sternly. "We're at church!"

"Sorry…was just pulling out my Bible app…I'll put it away."

His mom wasn't buying it but left him alone.

Evan took a final glance at his phone and sent a quick message to Gary before sliding it back in his pocket: "I'm in."

Chapter 4: Little White Lies

"I'll have the number six special," Evan said with a little bit of a pep in his voice, pep that he hadn't experienced for quite some time. There hadn't been anything this risky or exciting in his life since he and his friends decided to climb on the roof of the auditorium at college his freshman year during orientation. They'd wanted to see what the city looked like from that high up, and it was a beautiful sight. But it only lasted about 20 minutes until campus security found them up there after getting urgent calls from maintenance people in the auditorium, that there were loud thuds coming from the ceiling.

After a round of intense questioning about marijuana use (maintenance had found a blunt on the roof a few weeks earlier), which Evan and his new friends vehemently and truthfully denied, they were let go with a warning that next time there would be serious consequences. Since Evan was a good kid at heart, having grown up with strong Christian values, getting caught was enough to deter him from making any particularly devious choices for the rest of college. And he'd never really hung out with those friends again. Wonder what they're up to now? he thought. Maybe they'll be at 'polooza.

"Alright, the waffles, good choice," the waitress said as she scribbled on her green order pad. "How'd you like your eggs?"

"What? Oh, uh, over easy."

"Will do," said the waitress with a name tag that said Charlotte, and she continued down to his old church friend Christine, the next in line in their group of nine getting brunch after church per their weekly Sunday routine. Although this time, Evan had the particular privilege of being the additional, only-person-not-in-a-couple and thus uneven ninth wheel in their usual group of eight. It didn't faze him, though, because his mind was elsewhere, trying to sort out the millions of texts from Gary that were blowing up his phone now that he'd capitulated to temptation and agreed to go to Lollapalooza.

He was a little afraid to keep openly pulling out his phone with some of the risqué things that Gary had been sending for the last hour — pictures of girls that said "I love Lollapalooza" written across their boobs, some very NSFW gifs that made it explicitly clear what Gary's intentions and motivations for going to the festival were, and the ever-so-subtle, "Bro, we are totally gonna get you laid!!" The corners of Evan's mouth turned up as he tried to imagine the utterly embarrassing ways Gary might introduce him to women at this festival. Gary had a list on his phone that he'd been compiling for the better part of a year full of pick up lines to use both for himself and as a wingman for someone else and there was no way he wasn't planning to use them at the festival. It was his only move, and the most recent one Evan could remember seeing was a whopper - "Have you ever been arrested? It must be illegal to look this good - followed up by the suggestive, "Wanna do something that could get us arrested?"

God, please don't let him use that one for me, Evan half-seriously, half-jokingly prayed.

"What's so funny?" Christine asked with a curious smile. She was keenly observant in general, and especially to the fact that Evan kept looking down at his phone and chuckling every two minutes.

"What? Oh, um... funny cat pictures. Yeah, my mom has discovered the deep dark hole that is cat pictures and videos on the internet. So she's going a bit bonkers sending them." Evan chuckled nervously, hoping she hadn't seen what Heavy in fact had been sending.

"Oh, let me see them! I love cats," Christine chirped, reaching for Evan's phone.

"No! No, no, no," he said a little too aggressively and loudly, before clearing his throat and lowering his voice back down. "Uh, sorry, ah, no, ah, she sent them on Snapchat, sorry, sorry, so they already disappeared. But the next one I'll show it to you for sure."

"Your mom uses Snapchat?" Christine asked with a raised brow.

Shit, caught, he thought, but before he could dig himself into a deeper hole, he was rescued by Christine's boyfriend, Jake, who inquired about the up-coming Christian music festival.

"Yo, dude, you're coming to Florida with us right? We're all buying our tickets soon, so we should try to coordinate and buy seats next to each other!"

"Oh, man, I, ah, I totally wish I could come, bro. But my dad is actually paying for me to go to this financial convention in Las Vegas that same weekend. I have to take a test to prove that I actually learned something in school and won't screw things up if someone hires me to manage their finances. You know, that adulting life thing." And right away, before Jake could answer, he further thought, *That should hold up, right? I'll just buy my tickets to the festival with my dad's card, he'll think I'm flying to Vegas... no one will know.*

But Evan's palms started to sweat at the risk and excitement of his little white lie.

"That sucks, dude! There's not another one coming up later that you can go to? This is like a once-in-a-lifetime thing! Emily's cousin got us VIP access so we can actually meet the artists there!"

For a second, Evan reconsidered his decision to go to Lollapalooza, thinking maybe he should just forget about it. It wasn't too late because he could just make something up to tell Heavy, or even tell him the truth. And besides, his parents would probably be even more thrilled about him hanging out with his Christian friends at a Christian concert that going to the convention. Not to mention, ever since he played guitar in the church band in high school, he'd dreamt of being able to meet Chris Tomlin, the rockin' singer from Grand Saline, Texas, who would be there in Florida.

Just as his resolve began to falter, Evan's phone vibrated yet again, this time with the extremely rare sight of a serious text from Gary. "No joke, Ev, thanks so much for coming with me Bro. I really need my wingman with me to help me score some hot chicks."

Evan knew that, buried in the facade of hedonism, Gary was really just trying to get over Susie any way he could, which explained his silly fixation with trying to hook up with any and all girls who would be willing. While he knew Gary would do this whether or not he was there, Evan also knew that his friend needed him, and that he was Gary's only hope of not doing something absolutely crazy or over-the-top illegal. He had committed to go, and there was no turning back now.

"Man, that sucks," Evan said to Jake. "I wish I could go, but my dad would kill me if I didn't go to this thing in Vegas. He's already bought the plane tickets and everything. But you absolutely have to take a picture of Chris Tomlin for me."

"Dang. We'll miss you bro. but for sure."

Jake let it go and for the next five minutes the table bounced around several topics before eventually leading to the particulars of the new job Jake had landed a few months ago. "Yeah, it's called 'Fight the New Drug.' I'm just helping out with their graphic design and stuff, but it's actually really cool. It's not Christian, but it uses science and stuff to show how porn hurts your relationships and your brain and stuff like that and has people share their testimonies of how porn affected them and stuff. Yeah, so I can get you all free t-shirts, I actually have some in my trunk right now! You can all sport 'em and get people asking questions about how porn is harmful and stuff. "

Pride was beaming off of Jake so Evan joined the rest of the table in praising him for his work, but inside it caused him to feel a pang of guilt at his own habits of watching porn much more often than he cared to admit. He wondered how many other people at the table were feeling the same. And how hypocritical would it be for him to wear a shirt that says, "Porn kills love," when he himself was losing the struggle against the devil's temptations that went as far back as Adam and Eve.

Evan's mind was taken back to his philosophy class his sophomore year. "Is it more moral to fully and honestly admit who you are," he remembered the professor asking, "and the actual working values you live out, or to aspire to certain values that you aim to achieve but may never grasp or fulfill in their entirety through your own actions? In essence, is it immoral to say you believe something that you don't live out?" It was tough question then and is a tough question now. One he would not yet allow himself to answer, for fear of the truth.

A plate full of steaming waffles plopped down in front of him, shaking him out of his philosophical rabbithole. "Waffles for you, and your eggs and bacon are on their way," Charlotte said in her low sing-song voice. Too hungry to think anymore, Evan resolved to just take the shirt and decide whether or not to wear it later and focus now on eating He picked up his napkin and put it gracefully in his lap, grabbed his fork and dug in, having once again put off an important philosophical decision by making a practical one.

Chapter 5: Delilah

"Bro, I can't believe you're wearing that dumb shirt right now." Gary looked Evan up and down with disgust as he shuffled toward the airport check-in counter, a duffle bag in either hand.

Evan would agree, but had decided to not care about the moral philosophical implications of his clothing choices and just wear it as a sort of roundabout reminder to himself not to get entangled in too much trouble this weekend.

"It's comfy and I'm only wearing it on the plane. Plus, it automatically makes you look cooler if you're standing next to me," Evan said as he lifted his bag onto the luggage scale and flashed his ID to the woman behind the ticket counter.

Gary scoffed and grunted out, "Hm, I guess that's true. But that better not make a single appearance at the festival this weekend. No one is gonna wanna get with you while you're wearing that."

"Bro, this weekend is about you, remember? Don't worry about me. I'm just here for the music, food, and the bromance." Evan bounced his eyebrows up and down and put on his dorkiest face as he opened his arms wide to squeeze Gary into a hug.

"Alright, alright, get off of me! Save that for the ladies," Gary said, rolling his eyes.

The pair walked up to the line for security check, and after what felt like forever, made their way to their boarding gate, stopping at the overpriced convenience shop for a couple of snacks on the way, eventually plopping down on some uncomfortable blue chairs next to the nearest outlet. Evan pulled out his phone to charge it and began searching to see what he wanted to download for the flight. A little music definitely, maybe a few episodes of *The Office* off of Netflix.

His heart started beating faster as he caught a glimpse of the secret folder on his phone that he used to hide things he didn't want anyone else to see. He knew he had some porn on there that he'd downloaded in the past, but felt like it would be pretty damn hypocritical to watch porn on the plane given the attire he'd picked for the day. *God, help me make the right decision.* All the facts about the harmful effects of porn that Jake had been so casually spouting off during brunch were swarming through his brain. But it was so difficult to actually resist. *F it, I'm just gonna delete it. I don't want to be the creeper that watches porn on the plane anyway.* Before he could change his mind, he held down the icon for the secret app for a few seconds, selected delete, and breathed a deep sigh of relief as it disappeared into the ethernet.

Thirty minutes later the guys were settled into their seats. Evan was particularly happy and smug to have randomly scored the window seat when the clerk fixed their tickets, leaving Gary, not looking too happy, sitting in the middle seat on a full flight with a beefy guy next to him on the other side. Evan put on his headphones, selected one of the The Office episodes he'd downloaded, propped his phone up in the net basket on the back of the seat in front of him, then nestled his head into his travel pillow pressed against the window.

He only caught the first few minutes before dozing off, and before he knew it, Evan was waking up to the sound of wheels bouncing on the tarmac as the plane landed in Chicago. And though he woke up feeling a bit queasy in the stomach, he felt the indescribable peace of knowing that he had made the right choice and even gotten some sleep in instead of consuming the lurid contents of the now-empty secret folder (which he probably would have watched the moment Gary conked out).

The guys made their way off the plane, through baggage claim, and stepped outside into the hot Chicago summer air. The airport wasn't as busy as Atlanta, but there were still a good deal of cars weaving in and out and the place overall was packed to the hilt. O'Hare was known as one of the busiest airports in the United States and today was no exception. With taxi cab queue a mile long, Gary had tried Uber to see if it was allowed at the airport and it was, unlike some cities. $50 and nearly an hour later they were pulling up to Grant Park, the sites of the festival.

They got out of their Uber and Evan noticed that Gary gave him four stars. "Why not five?" Evan asked. "Not gabby enough for you?"

"Naw, I prefer quiet," Gary replied. "But I thought he was weak in the traffic. I would have taken a few side streets. Don't take side streets, don't get five stars."

Evan smiled and slung his bag on his back and they merged into the crowd to make the long hike onto the concert grounds. The place was buzzing with excitement and general insanity that Lollapalooza was renowned for, and before you knew it, both of the guys were flashing beaming smiles, caught up in the affecting festival energy. And the closer they got the more overwhelming it was, as the place had been transformed into a small city that had been tilted-up in a matter of days. Everywhere you looked there were heads bobbing, hundreds of thousands of them, with tents erected as far as the eye could see, smoke drifting up from BBQs, and undoubtedly every drug known to man or woman already being consumed.

"I've never seen anything like this before," Gary said, clearly in awe.

"Me neither," Evan replied. "It's like something out of a movie."

The guys trudged on until they found their reserved spot. They pitched their tent, loaded everything inside that they weren't going to take with them, then unfolded a big site map.

Gary pointed to one of the stage symbols on the map and said, that stage is all Alternative Rock.

Evan pointed to another stage. That's hiphop, R&B, and—

"Soul," Gary picked up. "And not too far away, over there" - his finger swept across the map - "punk and there electronica—"

"Then," added Evan, "country way back there." He swung his arm around and pointed to a big flag with a cowboy hat in the far distance. Then he said, "shit, look what's so close to us."

"What?" said Gary. "What?"

"The heavy metal stage, you know, devil horns and all." Evan flashed Gary the devil horns with his right hand, pinky and index finger stiff, center fingers folded down. Like what you saw Ozzy doing in every picture he ever took.

The long silence followed until Gary said, "well, I like those guys, Five Finger Death Punch."

"No you don't," said Evan, feeling inspired to explain why death metal and all those devil worshipping bands were corrupting the souls of America.

"Hey, forget it for now," Gary said. "Let's get a plan and have some fun!"

After circling and prioritizing some choices for that night, they took off for the beer canteen. "Two Buds," Gary said, slapping a ten-er on the counter. And before they knew it, they were immersed in the massive festival grounds swarming with a sea of heads that looked like an endless flock of gulls from the Aegean Sea back in the time of John of Patmos.

Then just as Evan finished off his first beer, the weirdest images started flashing across his line of vision in the general direction of the heavy metal stage, rising above the endless tents and throngs of people. Despite blinking his eyes rapidly because he thought he might be "seeing things," he couldn't shake away the bizarre shapes forming in the shape of images from the Book of Revelation. A seven-headed dragon was rising in front of the stage and not far away clouds were floating across the grounds in the shape of seven angels holding bowls outstretched in their hands.

His heart and mind in awe, he wondered to himself, could it be that I'm seeing what John saw in his vision when he wrote Revelation all that time ago? Pastor Jacobs said that God speaks to us in mysterious ways. Could this be it?" And before the images melted away, he could swear on a stack of bibles that he heard the voice of Jesus (or a male voice that he imagined must be Jesus), saying, "Son, I am coming and there will be a Judgment Day. I am coming, so prepare your life and make your decisions accordingly…"

For a moment he thought the vision and the voice must be the product of the beer, the sunshine, and the almost mystical atmosphere of celebration in the air, whereby he was deeply feeling, simultaneously, both a sense of spiritual ecstasy and a deep anxiety. It's not that he was a sex addict or something, but as a young man with raging male hormones he had guiltily sought the pleasure and truly wanted to meet a young lady and get laid, to do the real thing, as Gary had been talking about the whole drive there. Now he was stopped in his tracks, because he knew that sex before marriage, strictly speaking, was a mortal sin. Now the dark cloud of guilt would be hanging over him the whole concert.

And making it worse, the festival had just begun and they had tickets for all four days with plans to sleep in their tent all three nights and have a great old time, including some moments that might not be remembered ;-). Now his mind was torn between having loads of fun and lots of beer and chasing girls or abstaining from the "desires of the flesh" and staying pure, as the Apostle Paul would encourage. He knows that in the past he had succumbed to porn or having sex outside marriage, but recently he had been doing better to get his thoughts under control. Now he has this throbbing dilemma, no pun intended.

He and Gary set upon the concert grounds and took in the experience, visiting various stages, watching the opening bands, eating hotdogs and burgers and drinking more beer, until by sunset they are sunburned and tired. When heading back to their tent to take a nap, Evan bumped into a girl who immediately caught his fancy, spilling half of her fresh New Moon on the ground. She was attractive with light brown shoulder-length hair, big green eyes, and a bright smile on her face.

"I'm Evan, what's yours?" he said extending his hand to shake hers.

"Nice to meet you Evan, I'm Delilah."

"Sorry about that beer. Can I buy you another?"

"You sure can."

Chapter 6:

There's nothing like the feel of a vast music festival, especially Lolla-palooza. First, in the distance the highrises of Chicago rise into the sky like monuments to God. Then there's the endless sea of people, girls in tank tops, hair blowing in the wind. Boundless energy. Colours. Lights. And as it gets dark, rays of light. And asserted throughout, kids smiling as they stab devil's horns into the sky, in ecstacy.

"I went to Maranatha High School," Delilah says, "just around the corner from my church. We were always rivals with this school named Bethany down the street. We always demolished them in football," she laughed a smug laugh as he circled around and finally found a dry soft spot of grass to sit on as they sipped their beers.

"What the heck! That's my school!"

"You're kidding!"

"Nope. And I'll tell you this. You guys may have had the better football team, but we stomped you into the dirt in everything else." He was teasing but thought he'd been a bit too jock. She ignored it and rolled her eyes playfully.

"Ha ha, well," he said. "I didn't realize I had a Gladiator in my midst! I guess we can't be friends now."

"Only mortal enemies," she replied, raising her eyebrows. Then she slowly started to get up but didn't resist at all when Evan took her hand and pulled her back down, this time a little closer to him. He didn't know what caused him to do it, he just did. Like instinct or something.

Still holding hands, they locked eyes for a few seconds until Evan started feeling self-conscious and clumsily broke the silence. "So, um, ah, what church did you go to?"

"You assume I did go to church. Not everyone does, you know."

It caused him to pause, as this option hadn't even occurred to him. What if she's not religious. A pagan or something, he wondered.

"Ha!" she said. "Got you...No, I went to our Lady of Sorrows on Avalanche. I still go there every Sunday...But I mean, it's not *that* serious. I just go to listen to the homily and see some of my friends. What about you? What church are you at?"

"Faith Community on Lockwood." He wondered if she was hedging her faith in case he wasn't into it. A lot of the kids weren't. They attended church as kids but dropped it out of their life in college, turning instead to the pleasures of the flesh.

"That's cool," she said. "How often do you go?"

The truth was that Evan went to church every weekend as well, but had also been trying to take his faith more seriously by embracing his faith during the rest of the week. But he liked her and didn't want to scare her away by coming across as a holy roller or too uptight about it all.

"Same as you. I go on Sundays but mostly just to see friends."

These were innocent little lies, he felt. It's not that he was misleading her. He just wanted not to offend her before he know better where she stood.

He sensed a faint hint of disappointment in her reply, "Oh, okay," almost as if she were wishing that he attended church more often. But he wasn't sure. He also wondered if maybe she'd held back on admitting how seriously she took her faith, just like him. Then after a few awkward moments of silence, she declared, "Oh My God! We're actually at Lollapalooza. We have to take a freakin' selfie!"

Delilah quickly whipped out her phone, going straight to Snapchat, and for the next who-knows-how-long they tried on different Snapchat filters and Evan noticed her putting her face closer and closer to him until their cheeks touched. He felt good that she'd felt okay putting him on her story and soon noticed that she was getting loads of DMs from her friends in response.

After what felt like a few seconds but was really a few hours, the beautiful burning orange and pink hue of the sunset caught Evan's attention. He glanced at his watch and realized it was almost time for the Childish Gambino performance to start for the night on the main stage.

"Oh shit!" he yelled. "It's almost nine. We gotta go!"

"Hmm," she said. "I don't know about you, but I'm going to the Ariana Grande performance! You coming?"

"What? Seriously? Heck no, I'm going to Childish Gambino… I can't believe you listen to her!"

"She speaks to my soul," Delilah whispered only half sarcastically.

"Ha ha, alright, alright, well, I have to get going. I guess I'll see you around?" He gave her an awkward hug and started walking away backward, still looking at her.

Their time together had been so perfect that he was afraid to get her number for fear of disrupting the magic. If he left her now, this time would forever be perfect. She would be engrained in his memory as the most perfect girl he had ever met. He was also fearful of spoiling his impression of her, afraid of pursuing things more and then discovering she wasn't as perfect as she appeared to be.

"Yeah, I guess I'll see you around then," she said as she waved goodbye with a slight look of disappointment on her face.

They moved further and further away from each other, each looking back to get last looks of each other, and soon they couldn't see each other at all through the surging crowd.

As Evan made his way to the Childish Gambino stage, he was kicking himself for not getting her phone number or even her last name. Did she give me her last name? he thought. Gosh, he couldn't remember. What was he thinking, anyway? Here he had come to this festival to have fun and let loose, and meets this most amazing girl and he can't even manage to get her number.

He grabbed another beer and tried to shake away his regret by losing himself in the whole atmosphere of the festival. When he finally got to Childish Gambino he saw Gary, who blurted, "Bro, where have you been? I figured you would have been back in our tent area by the time I woke up from my nap!"

"Oh, I've just been with Delilah."

"Delilah? That girl with the amazing ass?"

Evan felt kind of embarrassed but laughed and said, "I guess."

"So are you guys meeting up later?"

"Actually, I didn't get her number."

"Bro, you can't be serious? What happened, did she ditch you?"

"No, no, I just forgot, well, didn't feel right. Just leave it alone, okay? Maybe I'll run into her again, and if not it wasn't meant to be, you know, then it wasn't meant to be."

"Whatever dude. You're crazy...Oh my gosh, there he is!"

Childish Gambino took the stage and the crowd went insane, allowing

Evan to take his mind off of Delilah for a while and enjoy the music.

But as soon as the show was over, he checked his phone to see if he could find her on Facebook, but after looking up every possible spelling of her name, and checking out profiles of people who he knew couldn't be her, but he checked just in case, he came up disappointed. He decided to numb his sorrows by just surfing through Instagram stories, and immediately realized that he'd forgotten he had his Instagram notifications turned off, because there in his DM's sat a message from Delilah from two hours ago. "Hey loser. Good thing I'm smart and found you in my suggested friends otherwise you'd be missing out on all this" followed by the emoji of a woman dancing and the fire emoji."

Maybe it *is* meant to be, he thought. He asked her how the Ariana Grande concert was and she replied snarkily, "A lot better than your concert, I'm sure!"

"Ha ha, whatever, but I don't think so." He posted up a pic of Gambino and then replied, "You hungry?"

An instant later she replied, "Starving."

Chapter 7:

There are certain girls that do that to you, aren't there?

This is what Evan was thinking as he weaved through gobs of people to find the other main stage where Ariana Grande had just finished, i.e., where Delilah was waiting for him. He'd told her to stay put and he'd find her near the big crazy flag that marked the food tents area.

They make your heart beat like you'd just run the hundred-yard dash, those girls. It's not like you said, hey, body, hey, heart, please go crazy and fibulate like a madman. It's when your heart takes on a mind of its own and drives you to do something, moving your feet, directing your chin, controlling the movement of your eyes.

You're like a hawk or owl, a bird of prey, looking for the next meal. Except it's not a meal, it's a girl, and you're not a hawk or owl, you're a young guy flush with raging hormones that hijack every part of you. And it's uncanny, because you can't control it no matter how hard you try. At least he couldn't, he thought, as he bumped into a stranger in his maniacal charge to find Delilah.

When he couldn't find her he messaged her and told her to go to the canteen with the goofy burger guy pasted in a graphic on a huge balloon that was bouncing and jerking wildly about ten yards high in the wind. You couldn't miss it if you were anywhere nearby. He stood there, holding the metal gate to which the balloon cord was tied, glancing back and forth to his phone, wondering if maybe she had changed her mind.

Several girls passed that at first looked like her but they weren't. The one had a low cut tank top showing herself too much.

"Evan, you okay?" a voice said, causing him to jump and turn toward the voice behind and over his right shoulder.

"Oh, Delilah, hi, I couldn't find you."

He blushed but that quickly went away when she pecked him on the cheek and hooked her arm around his. She obviously didn't notice his boner, or if she did, she didn't care.

"Hey, I'm parched and I was reading about those Aperol, ah—" she pulled up the concert program and looked at a folded page. "—Aperol Spritz drinks. They're at the Italian Social Club. Wanna get one?"

"Sure, sounds good. I'm sorta getting burned out on beer anyway." He partly said that to look good, like he wasn't a big boozer, because he didn't think she was one, most women were not big boozers, some were, most weren't, and she most definitely was not. At least that was his initial assessment, because if she was she'd already be way drunk. They were at 'palooza. Besides, it did sound responsible and that's how he wanted to come off.

"Or we could go to the Cupcake Vineyards Frozie Factory for one of those killer cocktails with foam all over it," she said. "My friend Susie was raving about it. I think she might have had one too many!"

Deliliah let out a big laugh and he wondered if maybe he was wrong about her. She did seem a tad tipsy and was being totally uninhibited, putting her hand around his waist, playfully grabbing his butt, stuff like that.

"Sounds good to me," he said. "Whatever you want is good with me, really." And this was true. Really true. Whatever she wanted, he was game.

"Yeah, let's do that instead," she said, stopping abruptly to get her bearings. "I think it's—" She spun around on her toes, tiptoeing up to see over the taller heads around her.

She was short, well, not short short, but about five foot four or five, he'd guess, and he was nearly six foot. About five ten and a half truthfully but six foot with any kind of heels. It's one of the white lies he told. He didn't know why, but he did usually add quickly at the end, when he was giving his height, "six foot, *with shoes.*"

She grabbed his hand and like a bird dog honing in on its target led him through the crowd with clear purpose until there it was, the Cupcake Factory display sign, with a huge line snaking around and around.

"Deliliah!" Someone yelled.

"Susie!" Delilah yelled back then turned to Evan. "Oh, gosh, how lucky are we. That's my girlfriend and look she's almost at the front. I knew she was downing those things. Come on."

They joined Susie and her crowd to the look of a few frowns from others in the line but like you do at crowded events you don't care about cutting line unless someone makes a total stink about it and no one did.

A few minutes later Evan, Deliliah, Susie and several other girls, one cute, one sorta ugly, chubby, actually, not ugly - he scolded himself for thinking that - were all standing in a small circle with two drinks each, one per hand so they didn't have to stand in that daggone line again.

"What do you do, Susie?" Evan asked, not sure why. Probably because he was always friendly and curious but here maybe more out of nervousness, thinking if she liked him and she was Delilah's friend then maybe that would make her like him more. Convoluted thinking but guys she did think that way. It came natural, at least for him it did.

Susie snorted and blue drink shot out her nose like water from a garden hose when you turn the spicket not expecting it, causing everyone to bust out laughing. He couldn't understand why everyone laughed at first.

He hadn't said anything funny. Then he realized everyone but him had glassy eyes and obviously had been puffing on some blunts. They were all high as a kite. Might even be X. Or one of the red or blue pills he'd seen exchanging hands in the crowd.

At about this time Susie, who must have noticed Evan's disconcertment, fingered a blunt from her pants pocket and swiftly lit a Bic lighter, taking a puff.

She smokes, he thought, surprised but not surprised, in the way you are when you meet someone new and get to know them better.

She held back a cough and passed it to him, at which point he froze and just looked at her hand. He did not normally imbibe, it wasn't his thing, made him feel weird, but he didn't want to make Deliliah think he was a square. And it was 'palooza.

"Ah, sure," he said, taking the blunt with pinched fingers and moving it to his lips. He sucked on it for a moment but it was almost out and he didn't get much smoke. Which was good, because he didn't cough. In fact, he pretended he got more than he did, just to be cool.

Because he didn't imbibe usually, even this little toke gave him a dizzy silly feeling all over, so when the cute girl, whose name he never got, took off and the girls followed he followed too, reaching forward and taking Deliliah's hand when she held it out to him.

Sometime later that night, maybe around midnight, the roving group of girls and Evan found itself near the heavy metal stage. Satanic images were everywhere — on billboards, flags, tee-shirts, fliers. And just then, when he momentarily let go of Delilah's hand, it happened again, bringing him to an abrupt stop.

He saw more images of weird stuff formed from various shapes that his mind imagined he was seeing — configurations of clouds, people's heads, stuff like that. Then suddenly at a distance he saw three numbers being elevated by three kids or groups of kids, and the numbers were: 6 - 6 - 6.

He jaw dropped, because he knew what they numbers meant. Or he knew what he'd read. The three sixes - 666 - were an Angel sign indicating your thoughts were out of balance and that you were focusing too much on the material side of life.

Was God sending him a message to keep his faith, or was all of this the result of the puff or maybe someone spiked his Cupcake drink, because he was feeling a bit dreamy and woozy?

That night he slept alone, giving Deliliah a goodbye kiss when she and the girls wanted to go do some girly thing, Susie making it clear that it was a girls-only thing. It's not that she didn't like him, Susie. In fact, she was very friendly to him and gave him a big hug.

So he got the message and with the remaining battery strength on his phone messaged Gary and then his phone went dead. By now he was getting tired and he thought that, in light of the sign, maybe he should return to the tent, say some prayers, he had brought his bible, and call it a night. So that's what he did.

But he did try something before he fell asleep, if truth be told. When he was done praying, he found his charger and plugged in his phone, not hoping to find a reply message from Gary but hoping to find a message from Delilah. He then prayed quickly for it as he waited for the phone to charge.

When the phone lit up about three minutes later he quickly pulled down his push notices from the top of his phone to scan what had arrived. There was a bunch of stuff from the Palooza app that he and Gary had downloaded, but nothing from her or Gary and then—

"Shit! Shit, shit, shit!" He actually yelled it out inside his tent though he was there all alone.

The tent, by the way, was a three-man tent which was spacious for two guys so they had plenty of room to roll out their sleeping bags and still store stuff to the side. And even though Gary was probably getting laid somewhere, if he did return it's not like they'd be sleeping on top of each other.

Anyway, the reason he yelled "shit!" three times is that he could swear one of the push notices read, "6-6-6," but then when he went to find where it went he could not locate it.

You know how that happens? You see a message flash across your phone and then a few minutes later when you're looking for it you can't find it. You look on Instagram and Snapchat and maybe even your email inbox or your LinkedIn, for those who have one, but it's nowhere to be found.

Crazy shit. And it happens often enough to even be spooky. And this was spooky. Really spooky, because he was not longer woozy and he'd just prayed and if he were to be honest again...the numbers appeared just as an imagined nude image of Deliliah appeared in his mind's eye.

Now he had this bad thought again and it was dark and he was alone in the tent and you know where that could lead.

Chapter 8:

I'm not going to tell you how the night ended, not yet anyway.

But Evan did sleep in late until the tent started getting hot, around 10:30 or so. He had rolled over once and the ground beneath his bag felt cold from the night and there was a chill to the air that caused him to pull my covers tightly around my naked self, because he did sleep without any clothes on. He did that at home, too, and at college, most of the time.

But by 10:30 the sun had heated everything up and he needed to let in some air so he unzipped the tent and stuck out his head and took a deep breath, which felt good. A few people standing around had obviously not gone to sleep yet and looked rough at the edges, red eyes, disheveled hair, puffy faces, you know the look. There were fewer girls who had smeared makeup, too.

A thin layer of fog hovered over the lower part of the tent area he was on, giving it that Civil War battleground look that he'd seen in pictures and a documentary where they tried to replicate what it really looked like the morning after Gettysburg. He didn't know why a concert would remind him of a battlefield, but it did. Probably just the fog.

He wasn't a big coffee drinker but today he felt he needed one. The puff had made him feel cloudy the night before and now it made him feel cloudy the morning after. At least that's what he assumed. It could simply be that he'd gone to bed late and, oh, well, he'd forgotten until now. He did have four or five beers and those two Cupcake drinks. Shit, it was probably those Cupcake drinks.

He stook outside barefooted in the cold and wet grass for a few minutes, taking in the battlefield. That's what it was, wasn't it? A party hearty battlefield, and he could see others looking over the landscape thinking similar thoughts. It's not like anyone saw this every day. It was unique, even extraordinary.

"Hey, that you, Evan?"

He turned his head and couldn't find the voice.

"Dude, over here."

A shirtless guy was waving his shirt which caught Evan's eye but he still had to squint until he realized it was his friend Larry Edelstein from school. He was one of the jocks who got interviewed for cheating, or was it porn. A decent guy, compared to many of the rest. Maybe because he was a swimmer, not basketball or football. Those guys tended to be jerks.

"Hey Lar, what's up? I didn't know you were here."

"Everyone's here, what're you talking about. The whole third floor." He pointed to a group of tents that looked like his, greenish with a tall center pole. Real nice ones with lots of head room.

"Yeah, that's all us. Most of us anyway. We all bought tickets right when they went on sale. Eddy has a connect. You know Eddy?"

Evan knew Eddy alright. He was the jerk of all jerks and right away his heart started beating nervously. Eddy had once asked him to help him cheat on a test and he'd refused. Not just because he didn't know what would be on the test, even though he'd already taken the class, but because he wasn't a cheater.

Eddy didn't give a shit about that. He felt he could pick on Evan and saw him as an easy mark, someone he could bully, probably because Evan was a pretty friendly guy and was always willing to help others with chores or homework if he didn't have something else going on.

But Eddy, he came onto to Evan like he had some kind of entitlement, being a starting defensive player for the football team. Probably never had anyone deny him anything, on account of the fact he was six six two-hundred ninety pounds, and that was possibly a lie, or inaccurate, off season. Three-hundred twenty or thirty pounds was probably more like it.

"Yeah, I know Eddy," Evan said, not adding any other comment but feeling he wanted to get dressed and outta here before Eddy and the other horses started waking up. "See you around then," Evan added then ducked into his tent to change into some fresh jeans and a shirt.

He pulled a handful of shirts out of his duffle bag and held them up, looking at the choices. One was a Church Club shirt that he wanted to wear but he was on the fence. He didn't want to rub Deliliah the wrong way, again, didn't want her to think he was some kind of holy roller. So he chose a golf shirt instead, one that his grandfather had given him.

Evan quickly dressed, grabbed his toothbrush and paste and stuffed it in his pants pocket and slipped away from the tent area, just in time to avoid Eddy. He could hear Eddy's loud voice blaring something ridiculous just as he left the area, thankful he'd escaped without confrontation. Because you never know about Eddy. One day he was friendly, one day he was an ass.

Evan washed up and brushed his teeth then headed to the closest coffee outlet. After getting a latte and croissant he sat down at one of the tables, left hand thumbing through his phone apps to see if he'd received any messages from you-know-who. And sure enough, he had.

"Morning Evan! Want to have brunch at the Mexican place?"

"Sure, where's that?"

"Near the heavy metal stage, you know the one."

He stared at the message for a moment, the sixes and demonic images flashing across his mind, then typed, "sure, when?"

"Now."

"K, on the way."

What are you so worried about? he asked himself. A bunch of sixes don't mean anything. He shook his head as he liked to do to clear evil thoughts from his mind, erasing them if you will, like words from a grease board.

When he finished his coffee, he spread the festival map on the table and found the spot. Looking up for a landmark, he saw what he thought was the stage and a bunch of food booths that looked like the place. It looked like a bit of a walk and he remembered from last night that it was about 20 minutes or so. But it wasn't nearly as crowded now, either.

Walking in the general direction of where he thought Deliliah was, Evan started to wonder if he should come clean with her about his level of commitment to his faith. I mean, he thought to himself, what if she really starts to like me but she doesn't know about my faith, and then when I tell her or she learns, and she will learn, sooner or later, she doesn't like it.

He kicked the walkway, mad at himself for not being more forthcoming. His little white lies did add up and they could get him in trouble. The porn, the concert, and now his faith. That was a big pile of white lies, when you looked at them altogether. And now the three sixes, which also meant other things.

He stopped and googled the numbers to find what he'd also read before. There he found that the numbers also referred to the devil's work and porn and weird and bizarre cultish stuff. There were satanic things that had happened in history where the three sixes were implicated. He wondered if he should ask Delilah what she thought, but Christ, he hadn't even been honest with her about his faith.

Suddenly a hot flash gribbed Evan, because the thought crossed his mind that maybe the whole damn festival was somehow the work of the devil, with all its excesses, rampant drug use, profligate sexual encounters, and lack of faith. It wouldn't be that big a stretch, would it?

He reflected on his grandparents, parents, Christian friends, and pastor from back home, wondering what they would think if they knew he had lied and gone to Lollapalooza. It couldn't be good.

To fight off the guilt, he ambled over to the beer garden and ordered a beer, and besides, maybe he could use a hair off the dog. He wouldn't be the only one having a beer before noon. DBN was a running joke at school, meaning Drunk By Noon. It's not that he did it often, but if there ever was a time, this was it.

He ordered and quickly downed the beer, alleviating all his qualms over the sixes and Delilah and such and after taking a quick piss continued on toward the Mexican breakfast place, picking up his pace when he saw a message from Delilah, "where are you?"

"Coming," he replied. "Be there in 5."

When he arrived, he was surprised to see Delilah sitting with Susie and a guy that he didn't know, and the guy was sitting next to her, not next to Susie. He strolled up and she yelled out, "Evan!," when she saw him and they hugged but she still sat next to the guy.

Small talk ensued, Mexican breakfast burritos were ordered at the counter by the guy, and Evan, frankly, had to know who he was as he hadn't, oddly, been introduced. Maybe it's because he quickly got a call and stepped away and then when he returned he offered to get the burritos.

But now, since he hadn't been introduced at the beginning, it's as if everyone had forgotten about it. It's probably happened to you, you know, when someone is introduced without his or her name being given and then you never know the person's name and you need to ask for it but for some reason are embarrassed to ask, as if you'd already forgotten the name when you never knew it to begin with.

Evan did notice that the guy was very homogenous to Deliliah, in the way that husbands and wives and boyfriends and girlfriends, and even their dogs, tended to look like each other. There was an affinity between lookalikes that was uncanny, how they were drawn to each other, as if being drawn to themselves. Because looking alike didn't mean you thought alike or shared values.

Finally after the guy nonchalantly put his arm around Delilah in a friendly way for the unpteenth time Evan mustered the courage to ask, awkwardly, "ah, I'm sorry, I didn't get your name. You are?"

"Rincon," he said with a huge smile. "People call me Rinc."

"Oh, okay, hey Rinc. How do you know—" Here Evan swept his hand around the table as if there was a group of people even though was only the four of them.

"Oh, I've, we've" - he gestured to Delilah - "known Susie since we were, what, Susie?"

Susie swallowed the last bite of her burrito and turned her eyes upward in thought. "Well, since second grade. Actually, Delilah and I were in the same class, if you recall, and you were two years ahead of us."

"Yes, yes, that's right. You had Ms. Zadon for first grade, the hot teacher with the red hair. I had a total crush on her."

Delilah, Susie and Rinc broke out in laughter but Evan remained solemn, his mind concentrating on the fact that still no one had described the relationship between him and Delilah.

"How do you know Delilah?" Evan finally brought himself to ask.

Rinc once again put his arm around her except this time he pulled her tight and she reciprocated. Evan practically fell off the bench at the sudden realization, or thought, that they were boyfriend and girlfriend and that all of his actions had been, well, he didn't even know what to think.

The last thing in the world he wanted to do was to engage in any kind of adulterous behavior and in a panicked moment his eyes moved to their ring fingers, where he observed that both fingers were bare. Which flummoxed him. He didn't know what was going on, and almost wanted to apologize.

No one answered, which was weird, because usually when someone asks you a direct question, you answer it directly, right? But instead, a subtle smirk and darting glances dances across everyone's faces, and after a long silence where everyone looked back and forth to their phones, which was what everyone did anymore when there was nothing to say, Rinc stood and said, "well, gotta run. We're gonna hang near the indie stage all day so we can get as close as we get as close as possible to see Imagine Dragons headlining tonight."

When Delilah stood, Even thought, darn, this is it. She's taking off with her boyfriend and I'll likely never see her again. But that's not what happened, because the next words out of Rinc's mouth were, "Susie, sis, I'll see you guys later. Evan, nice to meet you."

His body turned to jelly as Rinc walked away, and when he looked to Delilah, her mouth was open in a big circle, full of surprise.

"You, you, you didn't know he was my brother, did you?"

"No. No one introduced him. I thought—2

Delilah and Susie burst out laughing.

"I thought he was your boyfriend!"

For some reason, the tension created by the whole Rinc episode brought Delilah and Evan closer together. They hung out all day with Susie and that night, without Susie, who had joined her other girlfriends. They had a wonderful time together, getting lost in the moment, moving from stage to stage, and eventually losing track and having far more beer than either should have had. Without really intending too, because when you're drunk, your feet always end up taking you someplace that you suddenly find yourself in, they ended up stumbling into his tent.

Evan immediately collapsed stomach-down onto his sleeping bag as Delilah clumsily attempted to close the zipper back up, which took about three times longer that it would a normal, sober human being. Delilah turned and collapsed on top of Evan, and he could feel her lungs expanding and shrinking with every breath. He tried to sync up their breathing, intentionally breathing in and out at the same time as her. He could feel himself getting stiff again, but decided to ignore it. He turned his body around so he would be face up, Delilah falling gently off of him and onto the ground, and he turned and faced her so that their faces were within inches. Her eyes closed, he examined the freckles on her face and the sunburn across her nose and forehead where it hadn't been the day before. She opened her eyes and then suddenly they were both caught up in each other, as if their gaze was a Chinese finger trap, the type that grew tighter and tighter and more difficult to get away the more you tried. Evan felt his palms get sweaty, partially due to the heat of their proximity, and partially due to the fact that he never would have imagined being where we was now, inches from Delilah's face, close enough to hold her, and to kiss her… but he knew that could lead to other things and he had decided ahead of time that he wasn't going to have sex with some random stranger while he was here. But here she was, and she didn't feel like a random stranger, she felt like a best friend that he'd known his whole life, but a best friend who he was learning more and more exciting things about every second. He quieted the voice of doubt in his head, and decided to just be in the moment and go for it. He moved his face a couple of inches closer to hers and kissed her, and to his surprise, she kissed him back. And you know what that leads too.

Chapter 9:

Since neither intended on having fornication with anyone at the festival, neither had brought any protection; and when they awoke in the morning to a brightly shining morning sun, Evan felt a pang of guilt — but not a hint of regret. It wasn't the most pious start to a relationship, but he wasn't about to complain, either.

God forgive me, and please let this work out, he prayed silently to himself as he looked at the beautiful woman next to him, not believing he was in his sleeping bag at Lolla Palooza with this most amazing girl. And though neither knew the thoughts of the other, if you could have crawled into their brains, you would have learned that both of them secretly wondered if this wasn't the love-at-first-sight fairy tale that they'd read about as kids.

As Evan reflected on the previous day's events — from meeting Delilah's assumed boyfriend, who actually turned out to be her brother, to playing the always dangerous *Never Have I Ever* game with her and her friends, to the unexpected unfolding of events last night, he was suddenly shaken out of his daydreaming by the realization that they were not alone in the tent. He sat up as quickly as he possibly could without waking Delilah up and looked to his right to find a naked, hungover Gary rolled up in a ball in his corner of the tent. He shifted his weight and nudged Gary's shoulder, first softly, and gradually more rough until he finally cracked open an eyelid and showed he was alive.

He smirked and chuckled to himself, before quickly shaking off those prideful thoughts. He thought back to the commitment he had made to himself to be more sexually pure and growing closer to God, which definitely didn't include sleeping with anyone at 'Palooza, hence the no protection situation. But… it was probably fine, right? Plus, Delilah wasn't just some random girl he slept with. She was different… But even so, he hadn't revealed to her who he really was. What if this *was* just a one-time thing? What if she didn't want to be with someone who was so "religious"? Maybe he could avoid talking about that for a while and just enjoy the fun while it lasted?

As Evan considered the consequences of his white lies and the potential of correcting them, he noticed Delilah start to stir. "Gary, could you put some pants on and give us some privacy so she can at least get dressed without your creepy ass here to look at her?" Gary rolled his eyes, but obliged, and a minute later he climbed out of the tent, making no effort to keep the tent from shaking and waking Delilah up.

She slowly opened her eyes, and at first a look of panic flashed across her face as her eyes darted around the tent, but when they found Evan, she immediately relaxed and cracked a smile. "I forgot where I was for a second, haha. I thought maybe I'd done something I regretted last night," she said sheepishly. Evan hesitated, but asked, "Well…. did you?" Maybe it was great for Evan, and he was hoping for something in the future, and making all these plans, and maybe the whole time Delilah was feeling guilty, or bored with him, or whatever else other thing she could come up with. How assumptive of him to even start making plans when she could want nothing to do with him after all this. Luckily for Evan, Delilah just shook her head, smiled, and responded, "The only thing I regret is that fourth beer… Everything else was pretty much perfect." Evan cracked a shy smile and reached out to caress her hand.

"Oh shoot!" Delilah shouted with panic, suddenly sitting up straight and looking around frantically for her phone. "What time is it? I was supposed to meet my roommate, she came with me to the festival. We're cleaning up all our stuff supposed to head out at 10!" Evan was one of those, I guess you could now call it old-fashioned, kind of guys who still carried around a watch instead of just depending on his phone, so he looked down and announced that it was 9:27am to be exact. "Oh my gosh!" Delilah jolted up, hitting her head on the top net of the tent where a collection of chapstick, flashlights, trash, snacks, and other random items lay, and began searching underneath the blankets and sleeping bags for her pants. She quickly pulled on her light wash jeans, which still had some beer stains from the night before, grabbed her shirt, and gave Evan a peck on the cheek before rushing out of the tent. She popped her head back in before leaving for good, "Hey. Last night was wonderful. Let's get together when we get back home." "Absolutely," Evan replied, trying his best to sound a balance of eager but not desperate. She left, and all of 20 seconds later he got a notification from his Google Calendar with an invitation to schedule a coffee the following Friday at 10:30am. *Accept.*

Evan was completely engulfed in the world of Delilah as he and Gary drove home from the airport later that evening, after catching a ride with the world's chattiest Uber driver and a plane ride that had a little, but not too much turbulence. They weren't texting about anything in particular, and especially not about what had happened last night, but were exchanging the typical texts, memes, and gifs that one does during the first few days and weeks of falling in love. She'd even sent him the song "Can't Wait" by ESTA and Xavier Omar, one of Evan's newly favorite artists… so, basically she was definitely already in love with him too, right? But even as they messaged back and forth, his mind kept creeping back to the things that he had been holding back from her, his friends from church, his parents, everyone. Did he want to keep living this lie? He felt knots turn in his stomach.

They pull up to Evan's driveway and Gary shouted out, "At least you got some, dude!" before screeching away like the show off he was. Evan rolled his eyes, and walked in his place, where his parents were not-so-conveniently already awaiting his arrival in the kitchen. "Was that Gary?" he dad inquired, "How come he drove you home?" "Oh, I just asked him to pick me up from the airport." Another white lie, Evan thought. "Well, how was the convention, son?" For a second, Evan considered spilling the whole truth out on the table... But as he felt his palms begin to sweat again, his heart beat faster, and his stomach twist and turn, he couldn't bring himself to do it. It was great, he admitted, and yes he did gamble but just the nickel slots because everyone else did and yes he learned tons about financial services and yes it's still the field he plans to get a license in. They seemed to eat up everything he was feeding them, but somehow, digging a deeper lie didn't seem to quell his stomach much. "Did you," his mom mom raised her eyebrows suggestively, "*meet* anyone while you were there?" Evan's face turns red "Actually, I think I may have…if it works out, maybe I'll introduce her to you." "I would love that! As long as she's a good Christian girl of course." *Was she?* Evan thought. *Am I even the 'Good Christian boy' that my mom thinks I am?* As Evan's anxiety began to quell at how to answer that question, he was luckily saved by his mom's best friend Carol calling, and his dad's bowels calling.

As the days and weeks went on, Evan expected for his parents to ask him more questions or prod him about the girl he "met at the convention" like they usually did about every other aspect of his life. But surprisingly they didn't, probably caught up in the world of who was doing what with whom at church and who was going to win America's Got Talent, the person who could swallow fire while doing gymnastics, or the little girl with the incredible ventriloquism routine. In the meantime, he'd actually been able to catch coffee with Delilah a few times, although he hadn't been able to bring himself to have another conversation about that night they'd spent together, or about his faith or hers. When he wasn't with her or video-calling her, he was usually procrastinating on studying for his financial licensing test next month by kicking it with Gary or catching up with his church friends who just could *not* stop talking about how great the concert and revival was. He'd managed to start praying more too, and using the Bible app to do some of those pre-made devotions. He was actually starting to grow closer to God and become more like Jesus in different areas of his life. But Delilah stayed his little white lie that was growing bigger and bigger.

One night as he was doing a devotional one of the scriptures he was supposed to read was Luke 8:17: "For all that is secret will eventually be brought into the open, and everything that is concealed will be brought to light and made known to all." He felt a deep knot in his stomach and knew that the Holy Spirit was convicting him about the lies he had continually been telling about Delilah. What's worse, it's not that he knew he couldn't be with her — he was just so scared to show her who he really was, in case she didn't end up being who he hoped she was. He knew the twists and turns in his stomach wouldn't go away until he brought her into the light and introduced her to his friends and family. He exited out of the Bible app and messaged her, "Hey… sorry if this is weird or awkward or anything… and no pressure AT all… but.. would you like to come to my church with me this Sunday? I just figure you could meet some of my friends, and maybe even my family. But no pressure if you'd rather not… Lmk." He shook his foot up and down nervously as he waited for her response, but felt a strange peace as the knots in his stomach began to dwindle. Thirty seconds later his phone dinged, and his furrowed brow softened as he saw her reply, "I would love to!"

Chapter 10:

"I'm excited to introduce you to my friends and family," Evan admitted to Delilah as they walked up the steps on their way into church, hoping he wouldn't freak her out with his eagerness. She turned to him and their eyes met, and her mouth curled into a warm smile, "Me too." Her eyes darted away and she opened her mouth with hesitation, before she shakily said, "Evan, actually, I have something really important I need to tell you." "Anything, what's up?" Evan replied. Is she about to break up with me? Is it because I'm too Christian? Not Christian enough? What if I'm coming on too strong? Dang it, why is this the place I decided to introduce her to all my friends and family. A couple of seconds passed before she began, "Well… I'm —"

It seemed out of nowhere that Evan's mom darted out of the aisle, arms outstretched and smile as wide as can be, "Evan! Is this your girlfriend?!" She embraced Delilah in a tight squeeze, while Evan and Delilah made uncertain eye contact. "Umm…." he tried to read the look in Delilah's eyes. Maybe she'll say it and I don't have to? Delilah with a coy smile chimed in with"Yes, yes I'm his girlfriend, we met at —" "Uhh we met at the financial convention!" he cut her off with a nervous chuckle. Smooth.

Evan's heart started beating faster and he felt like he was about to burst with happiness. What was she going to tell me then, if she wasn't going to break up with me? He smiled back at her and grabbed her hand, fingers interlaced and all. *I have a girlfriend. Delilah is my girlfriend,* He thought with a light, airy surprised and rested happiness.

Church was about to start and they got caught in the flow of migration to the pews. Whatever Delilah wanted to say would have to wait. An hour and twenty minutes later, they followed the flow of migration again outside the church to the grassy area, where the discovered several tables set up by volunteers during the service filled with steaming aromatic barbecue chicken, potato salad, bread rolls, and more. They got their plates and sat down with Evan's friends, but he noticed that she was unusually quiet and pushing her food around. "Everything alright?" Delilah kept pushing her food around silently. "I just… really needed to talk to you about something." Evan glanced around at his friends at the table and deduced that their presence wasn't really making a difference in their conversation, so he grabbed her hand and they walked over to the stairs, leaving behind their half-eaten food for the flies.

"What's up?" Evan's palms started to sweat again as he thought of all the different things she could be about to tell him. She's moving away? She things they should take things more slowly? She's cheating on him? Wants to date multiple people? The list of ideas in his head were endless but guessing wasn't going to bring him any closer to finding out what was going on. He looked up and his eyes caught hers, which he could see were now glossy with pre-tears.

"Well… I'm… uh… I'm pregnant."

Silence filled the space between them, thick as fog, as Evan processed the one option he hadn't thought of. The knots that had dissolved in his stomach reassembled, twice as strong as normal this time, and he couldn't seem to form any words. All the things that flashed before him at the concert suddenly came back into his mind and he found himself becoming dizzy and lightheaded, and gripped the stair above the one where he was sitting in an effort not to fall over.

"Well… are you gonna say something? I just dropped some pretty big news.."

Words started to collect in Evan's brain…He wasn't ready for this. He hadn't even been able to be honest with her about the most important part of his life so far… they'd never talked about how many kids they'd want, what they think about adoption, abortion, where they'd want to raise a family… What — abortion. Oh my gosh, what if she believes in abortion… He started panicking and blurted out, "Would you get an abortion?!"

"What?" Delilah's eyes had full tears now, and she ripped her hand away from his, jolting onto her feet. She shook her head and furrowed her brow, "I can't believe you would even say that. We're done!" She turned and ran down the steps and over to the parking lot, got in her car and drove wildly away, almost hitting some teenagers who were jaywalking.

How could I be so stupid? That's not what I meant… How am I gonna fix this? Oh my gosh… I'm gonna be a dad? Head in a fog, Evan decided to walk home rather than go back to the BBQ. After twenty minutes of walking, he heard someone yell "Hey loser, get in!" He turned to the left and saw Gary's sarcastic face smiling back at him. Evan got in the car but said nothing, still gazing off into the distance as he processed everything that had happened in the past hour, the past week, the past months. It was all coming to a head. All his lies, all his mistakes, were finally catching up to him. A couple minutes into their drive, Gary broke the silence "Bro… what the hell is going on?" "I… she…" he sighed and realized that he couldn't possibly tell Gary. He wouldn't understand. "Nothing. I just… nothing." "Dude, there's clearly something going on." "Yeah… uh, Delilah wasn't able to come to church with me today. I was just bummed." *Another white lie. Why not?* Evan thought. "Bro, you need to get over it… It's not as big a deal as," he gestured with his finger and circled Evan's face, "all of this. Chill out, bro." "Uh, huh. Yeah… I"ll be sure to do that." They drove another couple of minutes in silence until Gary pulled into Evan's driveway. As Evan got out of the car, Gary yelled out "Grow some balls bro! See you later," before quickly skidding out of the driveway and pulling away.

Not knowing what else he could possible do, Evan laid down in bed. Maybe he could get some sleep and wake up and make sense of everything. Hours passed and though he had tossed and turned and open and shut his eyes what felt like dozens of times, he hadn't gotten a moment of sleep. The knots in his stomach by now had tied upon each other over and over until they formed a brick that felt like it was pinning him down into his bed. *I need to talk about this with someone,* he thought. He remembered back to his time in his church in high school, and wondered if his old youth leader Tim would still be in town. They hadn't talked in awhile, but he was always there when he needed him and he knew he'd be able to get everything out without being judged.

He pulled out his phone and began to text "Hey Tim! I know it's been a while but I have a lot going on and I could really use someone to talk to and give me wisdom. Do you have time to grab coffee in the next few days?"

All of ten seconds later, he got reply from Tim that gave him the most hope he's had all day, "I'll pick you up tomorrow at 10."

The next day Tim pulled up and texted Evan, "Here!" and immediately Evan started feeling knots in his stomach and sweating profusely. He'd been holding in all of his secrets for so long, living under the burden of his lies for so long, and now the time had come to actually tell someone. He took a deep breath, reached out his shaky hand to open the front door, and walked out to meet Tim who was standing outside leaning against his car.

"What's up, man? I miss you. Thanks for reaching out," Tim said as he walked up to Evan and gave him a big hug.

"Thanks for saying yes," Evan said sheepishly.

"Of course. Starbucks?" Tim suggested.

"Sure, that sounds good."

They got to Starbucks and were lucky enough to find a comfy couch seat in the corner of the room. After ordering drinks, they sat down and there was a long silence as Tim waited for Evan to speak. But Evan was so nervous, he didn't say anything. Finally Tim decided to break the ice, "So...what's going on, man? Tell me what's up."

Evan's voice started off shakily as he began to pour out everything that he'd been feeling, starting off with the burden and the stress that he'd been under and then proceeding to the guilt that he felt and how far away from God he felt and how he'd been trying to figure out the right way to live...but that he'd been giving in to so many temptations. He talked about his struggle with pornography and lying, about going to the concert, about his visions of 6-6-6, and then finally about Delilah. He told Tim he thought he was in love but that he'd ruined it. He got her pregnant and didn't mean to suggest abortion, but that's how she took it and now she hated him, or maybe she did. He did not know. She just ran away crying.

Tim asks him, "So, what do you want?"

"What do you mean, what do I want?"

"I think you need to ask yourself what do you really want? Do you want to be free? Do you want to keep living under the burden of your lies and your secrets and your shame, or do you want to step into the freedom that God has for you? It's your choice, you know."

Evan took a second to think and after taking a deep breath, exhaled and gushed, "I want to be free."

"Alright then," Tim said with a warm smile. "We can work with that. If you're willing to take the steps to get free, God can take care of the rest. Can I pray for you?"

Evan agreed and Tim placed his hand on Evan's back and prayed. He asked God to take off Evan's burdens, to take away any shame, any fear, anything that's holding Evan back from being close to God.

As Tim prayed, Evan felt a warmth in his body, and physically felt a weight being lifted off of his shoulders. By the time Tim was done praying, Evan felt a lightness of being and a freedom in his spirit that was like rapture.

"Wow. Thank you," Evan said with a huge smile on his face that he couldn't contain.

"My pleasure," Tim said, patting Evan assuredly on the back. "Remember that God loves you, his grace is sufficient for you, and he forgives you. All he wants is for you to live the life he's created for you to live."

"Yeah, I just needed to be reminded of that," Evan admitted sheepishly.

"Love you, bro."

They hugged and Tim brought life back to focus. "So, now that we've found a true path, what are you going to do about Delilah?"

"I don't know, I mean, I don't want her to get an abortion. I'll keep the baby even if she doesn't want it. But what I really want is to just be with her and figure it out together, you know?" He paused and as he did a wave of panic spread across his face.

"Oh no — She mentioned before that her dad lived in LA… what if she moves? Do you think she would do that?" Evan began to panic again.

"I don't know," Tim shrugs. "You know her better than I do."

"Okay, I've gotta go! I need to go find her right away!"

He jumped up, grabbed his jacket, and rushed out the door, Tim close behind him. As they get in the car, Evan anxiously fumbled with his phone and called Delilah. It went straight to voicemail. He called again and again, but no answer. Then he pulled up Instagram and sent her a message, "Delilah. Please. I need to talk to you."

Tim dropped him off at home and they hugged and said goodbye. Evan got into his own car and rushed over to Delilah's apartment and knocked on the door. He cracked his knuckles nervously as he waited. The door opened and he saw Delilah's roommate who he met at Lollapalooza, standing in pajamas and slurping up some Top Ramen.

"Hey, um, is she here?" Evan asked earnestly.

"Delilah? I haven't seen her since yesterday. She just grabbed her phone charger and her laptop and left. I thought maybe she was going somewhere with you."

"No, she wasn't with me," Evan replied with sadness. "Thanks anyway."

"Anytime," Delilah's roommate said, closing the door with her foot as she took another slurp of her Top Ramen.

Feeling defeated and out of options, Evan got back in his car and drove home. All he could do now was hope and pray that God made a way for things to work out.

Chapter 11:

Days passed and still Delilah hadn't answered any of his calls or messages. One night as he laid in bed depressed, scrolling through Snapchat stories, he noticed that Delilah's story had a posting from just a few hours prior. Eagerly he clicked on her story, only to be disappointed that it was just a quick picture of a gray speckled cat. Then he remembered — she had told him about her mom's cat! Knowing this would maybe be his only chance to figure out where she was, he grabbed his car keys and headed to the place he had dropped her off after their first lunch date after Lollapalooza. Maybe it was her mom's place and he would find her there.

In the meantime, in his own mind he knew he had only one choice, and that was to come clean to this family, ask Delilah to marry him, and have the child. He had loved her since first sight and she hinted at the same, he thought. So he found peace in his decision, even if the timing of the question has been prompted by her pregnancy. It was still true and still the right thing to do.

Evan arrived at what he assumed was Delilah's Mom's house, and ran up to the door to knock. A woman answered the door and he realized that he didn't know who she was – mother, aunt, friend – because he'd never met her family. She had shared some pictures, but he couldn't place the face. He asked if Delilah was home and the woman said she'd gone to visit her Aunt on the other side of Atlanta across the train tracks.

When he asked if Delilah is alright, the woman gave him a hard look and seemed to connect some dots herself and asked, "You're not… Evan, are you?" He flushed at her words and said he guesses so, at which point the woman gushed that she was Delilah's other aunt and that Delilah had told her everything.

He practically fainted for the second time that day and once again was speechless until the words blurted out, "I want to ask her to marry me and I want us to have the child and live our lives for God." Wow, he thought, he hadn't been able to admit that to anyone he was close to, but here he was admitting it to a total stranger.

"Evan… Hey, that rhymes with heaven!" she chuckled, taking up a few seconds of the already precious and limited time he had, "Anyway, you better get a move on because she's gone to her aunt's, my sister's. She has some things over there that she's packing up." She gave him the address and he put it into his GPS and he thanked her.

Evan drove across Atlanta like a madman and was lucky to get to Delilah's aunt's house alive. When he raced up to the door and knocked, breathless, a man answered and looked at him with disbelief because Evan knew he must look like a crazy man. After he explained who he was and why he was there, the man introduced himself as Delilah's uncle and invited him into the living room. Turned out he was the pastor of Delilah's church and she'd confessed everything that had happened to him. To Evan's surprise, he wasn't angry, but exuded such an atmosphere of compassion that Evan was taken aback and any walls he'd felt the need to put up came down.

He heard voices coming closer from another room, and immediately identified that it was Delilah and her aunt. When Delilah saw Evan she equivocated between breaking into tears and flying into a rage of anger. But instead, Evan hugged her and confessed that he loved her, at which time she just began to sob with apparent happiness. As they embraced, Delilah's Aunt and Uncle silently left the room, leaving them alone. It was clearly time for Evan to step up to the plate and be a man, take responsibility for his lies and actions and, equally importantly, own his faith.

"I have a lot of things to say to you, but mostly I want to say that I don't want to keep up all the lies… I really want to live my life for God, every day, not just on Sundays… and I want to do it with you. I know that might sound weird, but that's who I am," he confesses.

But before he could continue, she interrupted, "That's what I want too!" "I was afraid that you wouldn't be interested in me if I showed you how much I really want to take my faith and everything seriously… and that fear led me to making some really dumb choices. We're here now and can't change what's happened… but I want to go forward making the choices God wants me to make… and I want to make them with you, too."

They both smiled, just looking each other in the eyes, and moments later burst out into simultaneous laughter.

"Man… So you mean if we had just been honest with each other, we could have helped each other grow closer to God instead of everything that's happened," he said, to which she replied, "How crazy is that?"

They chuckled again, and Evan knew what he had to do. He looked around the apartment until his eyes rested on a decorative bauble on a table, grabbed it, and walked over to Delilah. To her surprise, he dropped to his knee, and clumsily gave the speech he had not been planning to make.

"Delilah, obviously we've had a weird start, and all of this craziness that's happening now… But from the moment I laid eyes on you, from the moment we had our first conversation, I knew that there was something different about you. I've never met anyone who understands me like you, who is so natural for me to be open and honest and real with… Haha, except for some things, but we've gotten that into the open… I guess what I'm trying to say is… I love you. And I'm not just saying this because we're going to have a baby, although that definitely speeds things up a bit… But… I don't want you to move away. I want you, and our baby, to stay here with me, and…What I'm trying to say is…Would you marry me?"

He looked into her eyes, which were filling up with tears again, but he'd hoped it was the good kind of tears this time, and waited for what felt like minutes for her reply as she just stood there staring back into his eyes.

"Yes, but on two conditions: One, we both put God first in our relationship from this point on, and two," she paused and let out a laugh, "you have to promise that you're changing diapers with me."

Evan laughed and said, "Deal."

He placed the bauble onto her finger, stood up, and embraced her with the longest hug they'd ever had, and it felt like they were falling into complete and utter joy in each other's arms. When the long, long, long hug ended, they looked at each other and at the same said: "How are we gonna tell Gary?"